THE ISSUES
OF SURVIVAL

The Treaty Veto of the American Senate
(1930 and 1968)

The United States and
the League of Nations, 1918–1920
(1932 and 1968)

The United States and
World Organization, 1920–1933
(1938 and 1968)

Can We Win the Peace?
(1943)

While America Slept
(1944)

The United States and
the World Court, 1920–1966
(1945 and 1968)

The Cold War and Its Origins, 1917–1960
(1961 and 1968)

The Origins and Legacies of World War I
(1968)

America's Role in Asia
(1969)

The Issues of Survival
(1972)

THE ISSUES
OF SURVIVAL

D. F. Fleming

Emeritus Professor of International Relations
Vanderbilt University, U.S.A.

London
GEORGE ALLEN & UNWIN LTD
Ruskin House   Museum Street

First published in Great Britain in 1972

© 1972 D. F. Fleming

ISBN 0 04 330214 9

The British Edition is a photographic copy and American spelling and usage have been retained

Printed in Great Britain
by Redwood Press Limited
Trowbridge, Wiltshire

To the multitudes of our students who have seen clearly the urgency of economic, social, and military reforms—to prevent the early decline of overurbanized, corporate America—with the hope that they will continue to work throughout their adult lives to give us a reorganized, reasonably long national life.

CONTENTS

I. CAN WE AVOID THE FINAL WORLD WAR? 1
The Cold War and After.

Appeasement. Decisions During the War. East Europe Divided by Churchill and Stalin. Free Elections. Truman's Reversal of the Roosevelt-Hull Policy. The Truman Doctrine. Closed Corridor. Containing China. Obsessive Anti-Communism. World Community.

II. CAN WE AVERT THE EXTINCTION OF MAN? 18
Are Environmental Destruction and Overpopulation Controllable?

Three Explosive Forces: Nuclear Extinction? The Technological Explosion; The Population Explosion. Let Technology Save Us. How Much Time Do We Have Left? New Objectives. Our American Responsibility. What Can We Do Now? World Action Imperative.

III. WILL MILITARISM DESTROY THE UNITED
STATES?   35
Is the Military-Industrial Complex Manageable?

The Military-Industrial Complex. "Mad Momen-
tum." ABM and MIRV. Military Socialism. Other
Looming Perils. Vietnam Fiasco. Pentagon Rule
Challenged. Can Civilian Control Be Effective?
What Ways Out?

IV. CAN WE ESCAPE FROM CONTAINING CHINA?   55
How Can We Move Toward Making Peace?

The Korean War. Containing China. Vietnamese
Bastion: Johnson's Escalation; Nixon's "Viet-
namization"; Escalation into Cambodia. As the
World Saw It. Widened War. The Nixon Plan.
Corrupted Colony. Permanent Obligations. A
South Korean Solution? Why Vietnam? China's
Contribution. Self-Defeat. Cold War Collapse.
Can We Escape? Ten Steps Toward Peace.

V. THE RISE AND FALL OF THE AMERICAN
EMPIRE.   83
Can We Learn from History?

From Cooperation to Containment. Economic
Empire. Defeat in Vietnam. Our God Complex.
From World Power to Weakness. Nationalism As-
cendant. Internal Priorities Imperative. Can We
Reduce Our Apparatus of Empire?

VI. CAN WE HALT OUR INTERNAL DECLINE?   95
Must Our National Life Be Short?

Imperative Tasks: Where to Live? Mass Trans-

port; Ending Endemic Poverty; Neglected
Schools; Failing Courts and Prisons. The Corpo-
rate State: Reform of Congress Required; Is
America Finished? Youth Repelled; Back to An-
archism? New Consciousness Emerging; More
Thinking and Action from Below. Perils Shared
with the World: Overpopulation; Controlling
Pollution; The Final Arms Race—and Absurdity.
We Can Change Course.

PREFACE

Within the past three or four years a new and terrible realization has dawned on people everywhere in the world of developed nations, especially in the minds of the young.

Until then all thoughtful people had known ever since the failure of the United States to enter and lead the League of Nations that the Western world was most likely to be destroyed by succeeding world wars. This common-sense forecast was tragically fulfilled in World War II, with the added clincher that a new and easy means of ending all life on earth was invented. The atomic bomb was placed in the hands of two big governments which entered into what almost certainly would be the last arms race. Either it would end in the final war, or in a decision to move into a more dependable world order.

But just as there were signs of a stalemate in the race toward nuclear death, thoughtful men everywhere began to understand that the earth itself and our entire natural environment were being dangerously polluted, and that a fast-developing population explosion would accelerate the devastation of our really fragile spaceship earth.

Therefore, for the first time in all history the end of humanity itself became not only thinkable but apparently unavoidable, given the powerful forces promoting humanity's extinction that appeared to be uncontrollable.

It was the hope that this fate for our entire civilization might at least be postponed over a long period which led to these lectures.

Two early versions of them were published in 1969: "Will Militarism Destroy the United States?" in the November *Forensic Quarterly;* and "Can We Avert the Extinction of Man?" in the Autumn *Queen's Quarterly.* "Can We Escape from Containing China?" was published in the March 1971 *Western Political Quarterly.*

The first three lectures and the last two presented here were delivered at Vanderbilt University under the auspices of the University Lecture Committee and the Political Science Department. The fourth lecture was given to the Peabody College Seminar of the Robert A. Taft Institute of Government. All have been slightly revised since delivery.

They are offered as efforts to think through toward hope of continued human existence, no matter how drastic the solutions might be. Some of these point toward complete reversals of our ways of life that will be deeply shocking, "unthinkable" to many. But what is totally unacceptable now is likely to be embraced a little later, too late to save us.

D. F. Fleming

June 1971

THE ISSUES
OF SURVIVAL

I. CAN WE AVOID THE FINAL WORLD WAR?
The Cold War and After

The Cold War originated in the chagrin of Western leaders, notably Churchill and Truman, over Soviet control of Central and East Europe after World War II. When Hitler attacked Russia in June 1941, there was almost universal expectation of a swift and crushing Soviet defeat, and no one dreamed that after it was all over the Red armies would be in control of Berlin and Vienna.

Seeking scapegoats, many alleged that Roosevelt had given away Eastern Europe at the Yalta Conference early in 1945. This was and is a giant myth. It is not possible to understand the Cold War without a full appreciation that East Europe was lost to the West at the Munich Conference in September 1938, not at Yalta some seven years later.

Also it must always be remembered that at the time of the Yalta meeting no one wanted the Russians to stop driving the Germans back through East Europe, and that the Americans greatly desired Russia's help against Japan after the German war was over.

Appeasement. The Munich Conference was the cul-
mination of a long process of appeasing Hitler by turning
him toward the East. Throughout the three years of the
fascist conquest of Spain, beginning in 1936, the British
Government resolutely held the blanket of the London
"Non-Intervention" Agreement over the Spanish tragedy
until the Republic was slowly strangled to death. Then
Austria was publicly warned by Neville Chamberlain on
March 7, 1938, not to expect any help from the League
of Nations, and she got none when overrun by Germany
three days later.

For Czechoslovakia, the third democracy to be sacrificed deliberately, Chamberlain planned in advance to put
such pressure on the Czechs that they would never be
able to fight for their lives, thus preventing their French
and Soviet alliances from coming into operation. In this
he was sadly successful, at the price of three flying trips
to Germany to propitiate Hitler. "Of course they want to
dominate Eastern Europe," he had said of the Germans
as early as November 26, 1937,[1] and all of his acts resolutely
helped them to do so. By breaking down the mighty
Czech bastion for the Nazis he gave them Eastern Europe,
beyond any power to recall the gift by last-minute declara-
tions of support for Poland—in 1939.

Chamberlain and the pliant, defeatist governments of
France that he carried along with him did not intend
to turn East and Central Europe over to communism.
They delivered it to fascism, but after Munich in 1938,
it was never possible to halt the march of events until
the Russian armies occupied Berlin and Vienna.

[1] Keith Feiling, *The Life of Neville Chamberlain*, New York, 1946,
p. 333.

Decisions During the War. The inevitability of Russia's arrival in Central Europe, if Hitler was to be defeated, was not understood even in Washington in the early stages of the war. In December 1941 and February 1942 the Dunn-Atherton State Department memorandum reasoned that Stalin might not be able to recover all of his lost territories and ruled against recognizing his seizure of the Baltic states and half of Poland.[2] Our fear of another uproar over "secret treaties," such as had been raised after World War I, and of the outcry of Polish and other citizens, combined with aversion to any extension of the areas of communism to prevent the British from making a more realistic agreement with Russia in April 1942.

Then the British managed to lead Western war operations through peripheral warfare in North Africa, Sicily, and Italy until May 1944. This was justifiable strategy for us, but it left the main brunt of the land war on the Russians to the end and created in their minds lasting suspicions of being deliberately sacrificed. More important, it gave the Russian armies time to come into Central Europe, at the cost of many hundreds of thousands of lives, losses which we would have suffered had we struck sooner and directly at Germany.

All during the war years, Churchill sought manfully to retrieve in East Europe what Chamberlain had given away. Churchill's eyes were always on the non-existent "soft underbelly" of Europe, then in the late stages of the war on an invasion through Trieste, and finally for lunges into Germany to seize areas beyond the agreed zones of occupation for bargaining purposes. But always the actual balance of forces defeated him. The Russian armies were required to maul the bulk of the German

2 Cordell Hull, *Memoirs*, New York, 1948, Vol. II, pp. 1165–70.

forces to the last day of the war. Allied forces thrown
through Trieste might well have enabled the Russians
to skirt the Baltic Sea and appear on the English Chan-
nel. Furthermore, attempts to change the zones of occupation against the Russians would have been rejected by
Allied public opinion. Long afterward General Bedell
Smith, one of General Eisenhower's most trusted generals, recorded his conviction that it "would have been
quite impossible in the light of world public opinion and
in our own country," and his advice to Churchill at the
time was "that I didn't think his own public opinion
would permit it."[3]

Soviet control of East Europe was the price we paid
for the years of appeasement of Hitler, and it was not a
high price. In Toynbee's judgment "the Nazis would
have conquered the world," if we and the Soviets had
not combined our efforts. They would eventually have
crossed the narrow gap of the South Atlantic to Brazil
and the rest of South America, where strong German-
speaking fifth columns could have been organized in more
than one country. By our war alliance with the Soviets
we prevented the unification of the world by the Nazis.
That was a victory beyond price, but, says Toynbee, we
"could not have put down Hitler without consequently
producing the situation with which all of us now find
ourselves confronted."[4]

All this was fully evident during the war and it is still
true. C. B. Marshall has reminded us that we do not have
to guess what the Axis powers would have done had they
won. They set it down plainly in their Tripartite Alliance

[3] Walter Bedell Smith, "The Cold War—An Audit," The New York
Times *Magazine*, October 10, 1954, pp. 30–31.
[4] Arnold J. Toynbee, "What World War II Did and Didn't Settle," The
New York Times *Magazine*, May 1, 1955, p. 66.

on September 27, 1940—"a pattern for the conquest of the rest of the world and the beleaguerment of the United States."[5] Why then did we have ten years of Cold War over Russia's control of East Europe and over her desire to have a military base on the Turkish Straits?

East Europe Divided by Churchill and Stalin. Early in October 1944 Churchill sought to come to terms with the inevitable. Over the strong opposition of the State Department, but with Roosevelt's permission, he went to Moscow to make a temporary agreement for three months concerning the Balkans.

On October 9 he proposed to Stalin that Russia have 90 per cent predominance in Romania, others 10 per cent, and 75 per cent predominance in Bulgaria, others 25 per cent. In Greece, Britain would have 90 per cent predominance, and others 10 per cent. The "predominance" was to be divided 50–50 in Hungary and Yugoslavia. Nothing was said about this division of influence being temporary.[6]

Stalin accepted this proposal without a word. He permitted a really free election in Hungary, which the old ruling classes duly won, and he did his best to force Tito to honor the bargain about Yugoslavia.[7] Also he held his hand completely while Churchill promptly crushed the forces of the Left in Greece, thereby sealing his agreement with Churchill and committing Roosevelt to it before Yalta.

[5] C. B. Marshall, *The Limits of Foreign Policy*, New York, 1954, p. 72.

[6] Winston Churchill, *Triumph and Tragedy*, New York, 1953, pp. 227–28.

[7] Vladimir Dedijer, *Tito*, New York, 1953, pp. 232–34.

The Communist revolution in Bulgaria was already in full cry when the Yalta Conference met. The overthrow in the preceding December of the mighty ELAS movement in Greece, by the British army and the Greek officer caste, had suggested to the Russians that something very similar could occur in Bulgaria, where the Bulgarian army officers used the coup d'état "as a normal political instrument."[8] "People's Court" trials began on December 24, 1944, and cut down the Bulgarian army officers as with a scythe until the end of February 1945.

On March 6 the Soviet Government imposed a Communist-led government upon Romania, deposing the Romanian conservatives. It was "very hard to think of any constructive alternative," since free elections in Romania under their control would have been "an invitation to Fascism here more than elsewhere."[9]

The situation was worst in Romania, where government was notoriously "so corrupt that it was a synonym for corrupt government,"[10] but there was no country in East Europe, with the exception of Greece, where the kind of free elections we wanted would not have been controlled by the old ruling classes. They had manipulated the elections for generations. No free election had ever been held. The Hungarian landlords had been ruthless rulers for a thousand years, and elsewhere the cliques which ruled for their own benefit had virtually all of the knowledge of political manipulation. Hungarian and Romanian ruling groups had also sent 2 million conscripted troops into Russia, behind Hitler's armies.

[8] Howard K. Smith, *The State of Europe*, New York, 1949, pp. 351, 289.
[9] *Ibid.*, p. 364.
[10] Joseph C. Harsch, *The Curtain Isn't Iron*, New York, 1950, p. 48.

Free Elections. In these circumstances the question arises, why did Stalin agree at Yalta early in 1945 to conduct "free elections" in Eastern Europe? Why we demanded them was clear. That is the American way of doing things, subject to the operations of political machines, and we wanted very much to prevent East Europe from being communized. No one at Yalta thought of denying that the region must cease to be a hostile *cordon sanitaire* against the Soviet Union and become "friendly" politically to her. No one could deny that, with the Red armies at that moment across Poland, within thirty miles of Berlin, and beyond Budapest sweeping up the Danube, while the Western Allies were still in France, set back by the Ardennes offensive.

But could governments friendly to Russia be obtained in this region by "free elections" in which the ruling groups participated freely? It was inconceivable that these groups could be friendly to Russia, or that Communist Russia could think of depending on them. That was as incredible as that we should freely arrange for a Communist government in France or Italy. The Soviets also happened to believe that their system of government was as valid as ours, and that they could really depend only upon it to stop East Europe from being used as an invasion corridor into the Soviet Union.

If the Americans at Yalta committed a fault, it was not in "giving away" East Europe. That had been done at Munich long before. It was in trying to achieve the impossible under the formula of "free elections." Yet free elections were in their blood and they could do no other than to believe that this was a solution which all must accept. On his side, it is not likely that Stalin thought the formula would prevent him from purging the long-dominant elements in East Europe whose hostility to Red Russia needed no further demonstration. These elections might be managed, he must have thought, and "people's democracies" set up which would be acceptable to the Americans. He knew that the decisive settlement for the area had already been made in his gentleman's agreement with Churchill, on October 9, 1944, and that its execution was already far advanced on both sides.

He was loyally holding to his side of the bargain with Churchill and he could hardly have believed that the Yalta formulas would disrupt Allied relations as soon as the war was over and lead to long years of bitter Cold War.

Truman's Reversal of the Roosevelt-Hull Policy. It is possible that if Roosevelt had lived the same deadly quarrel would have developed, though it is far more likely that he already understood the deeper forces involved and the impossibility of frustrating them. What made a clash certain was the accession of Truman just at the close of the war. He intended to carry out Roosevelt's engagements, loyally and fully, and to exact from Stalin the same complete fulfillment, including free elections in East Europe. This theme runs through the first volume of Truman's memoirs.

However, his methods were poles apart from those of Roosevelt and Hull. All through 1944, his last year in office, Hull had conducted off-the-record conferences with groups of editors, clergymen, and members of Congress, to explain to them how far the Russians had come with us, how they had been "locked up and isolated for a quarter of a century," used to receiving violent epithets. It would "take time for them to get into step," but they would do it. He urged that "we must be patient and forbearing. We cannot settle questions with Russia by threats. We must use friendly methods."

No one was more opposed than Hull to Soviet control of East Europe, "interfering with her neighbors," as he put it, but as he left office his policy rested on two bases: to show the Russians by example how a great power should act, and to continue in constant friendly discussion with them. "Consult them on every point," he urged. "Engage in no 'cussin matches' with them."[11]

Nothing could have been further from President Truman's approach. He quickly read all the dispatches about friction with Russia over German surrenders, listened to everybody who wanted to get tough with the Russians, and when Molotov came by on April 23, 1945, to pay his respects to the new President, he received such a dressing down that he complained at the end of it that no one had ever talked like that to him before.[12]

This was exactly eleven days after Roosevelt's death. It took Truman just that long to reverse the entire Roosevelt-Hull approach to Russia and to inaugurate an era of toughness and ever greater toughness in our dealings with her. Then on July 16, 1945, our successful test explosion of the first atomic bomb gave him the means to back insistence on free elections in East Europe and when the London Conference of September 1945 deadlocked over this issue, Truman made up his mind at once to "contain" Russia.[13] It was at this moment that Walter Lippmann, noting that we had terminated lend-lease "abruptly and brutally" and drifted into an arms race

[11] Hull, *Memoirs*, Vol. II, pp. 1464–71, pp. 1406–8.

[12] *Memoirs by Harry S. Truman: Year of Decisions*, Garden City, N.Y., 1965, Vol. I, p. 82. This was a strong statement, since Molotov had lived with Stalin a long time.

[13] Arthur Krock, *New York Times*, March 23, 25, 1947.

with the Soviet Union, warned: "Let no one deceive himself. We are drifting toward a catastrophe."[14]

To the already deep fears of Russia for her own security, thrice justified since 1914, was added a new and dreadful fear of a fourth Western attack, backed by the atomic bomb. From the psychological point of view the policy of toughness was "the worst treatment" that could have been devised. "If a patient is suffering from genuine fear, you do not cure his fears and establish a rational relationship with him by making him more afraid. You endeavor to show him patiently and by your actions toward him that he has nothing to fear."[15]

Exactly the opposite course was followed, with increasing momentum. In the following spring of 1946 Churchill issued at Fulton, Missouri, and in President Truman's applauding presence, his call for an overwhelming preponderance of power against Russia, hinting broadly at later forcible interventions in East Europe. Nevertheless, peace was made in Europe during the remainder of 1946. In three sessions of the Council of Foreign Ministers and a conference of twenty-one nations in Paris, peace treaties were hammered out in substantially the terms established by the various armistices. Really free elections had been held in Hungary and there were many signs of relaxation of tension as the year closed.

The Truman Doctrine. However, in February 1947, the British turned the burden of supporting Greece over to us and Truman seized the occasion to proclaim the doctrine of containment, on March 12, 1947, which George F. Kennan spelled out fully in the July issue of *Foreign Affairs*

[14] *Nashville Tennessean,* November 4, 1945.
[15] Kenneth Ingram, *History of the Cold War,* New York, 1955, p. 228.

as "long term, patient but firm and vigilant containment of Russian expansive tendencies." Otherwise the Kremlin would take its time about filling every "nook and cranny available to it in the basin of world power."

On its face this was the rashest policy ever enunciated by any American leader. For the first time in history the encirclement of a great power was openly proclaimed. This power, too, was in firm possession of the great heartland of Eurasia. It had already demonstrated that it could industrialize itself quickly and enough to defeat Hitler's armies. What it would do, after the Cold War was declared by Churchill and Truman, was easily predictable. The Soviet Union would put up a bold front to cover its frightening postwar weakness and work mightily to gain strength to hold what it had and then break the encirclement.

This was a difficult undertaking, for not only was the Soviet Union frightfully devastated, but Eastern Europe was in nearly as bad shape. However, what the Soviet peoples had done twice already they could do again, under the lash of containment. After the two grueling forced marches, before 1941 and after the German invasion, they undertook still a third and within eleven years from 1946 they had achieved first their A-bomb in 1949, then the H-bomb in 1953 and the first ICBM in 1957. In all other vital respects also they had gained that position of strength which was our announced goal after March 1950.

In the course of containment, "negotiation from strength," and liberation, we revivified fully the machinery of totalitarian rule in Russia. As William A. Williams has pointed out: "Appearing as a classic and literal verification of Marx's most apocalyptic prophecy, the policy of containment strengthened the hand of every die-hard

Marxist and every extreme Russian nationalist among the Soviet leadership."

Containment also gave Stalin total power over the Soviet peoples. Williams continues: "Armed with the language and actions of containment, which underwrote and extended his existing power, Stalin could and did drive the Soviet people to the brink of collapse and, no doubt, to the thought of open resistance. But the dynamic of revolt was always blocked, even among those who did have access to the levels of authority, by the fact of containment and the open threat of liberation. Thus protected by his avowed enemies, Stalin was able to force his nation through extreme deprivations and extensive purges to the verge of physical and psychological exhaustion. But he also steered it through the perils of reconstruction to the security of nuclear parity with the United States."[16]

Closed Corridor. Throughout the Cold War it was never possible for the Soviet Union to relinquish control of East Europe, for the reason that Russia had been invaded disastrously through that region three times since 1913. During World War I, the Western interventions of 1918–20, and World War II the Soviets lost at least 30 million people and suffered property and psychological damage beyond the power of any other people really to comprehend. No great power which had suffered even one of these tragedies would have failed to hold East Europe as a security zone. If the West had made any effort to realize this, the Cold War could have been avoided.

Instead, Western promises of liberation and the back-

16 William A. Williams, "The Irony of Containment: A Policy Boomerangs," *The Nation*, May 5, 1956, pp. 376–79.

breaking pressures of the Cold War combined to make life almost unendurable to the peoples of East Europe until the Polish and Hungarian revolts of 1956 demonstrated finally that the West had no power to help the East Europeans.

The second Berlin crisis of 1958–59 demonstrated clearly that the military writ of the West does not run even to West Berlin. Months of talk about sending tank columns and airlifts ended in a realization that it makes no sense to destroy Berlin, Germany, and much else in order to "defend" West Berlin. This was the meaning of President Eisenhower's wise decision to try to end the atmosphere of the Cold War, to save as much as possible of the Western position in Berlin by negotiation, and of his efforts to arrive at a *détente* with the Soviets at the abortive summit conference at Paris in 1960.

Containing China. Eisenhower failed, due largely to the folly of sending a spy plane over Russia at this critical moment, only to have it shot down. Then the United States concentrated its efforts on maintaining the close encirclement of China, which had been achieved in the course of World War II.

This effort led into the morass of the Vietnam War, which has resulted in the death of some fifty thousand American troops, in combat or associated with it, and in the serious maiming of perhaps twice as many, along with the death of several hundred thousand Vietnamese, and the creation of millions of refugees. Several million Vietnamese peasants have been forcibly urbanized and an ancient, viable civilization very gravely undermined.

In the process American civilization has been shaken to its foundations, the nation divided, its frightening urban problems and its rural poor neglected, and the hopes of its black citizens frustrated. In mid-1969, 108 billion dollars had been squandered on the war, billions that could have made the U.S.A. healthy, on top of nearly a trillion dollars spent otherwise on the Cold War that could have made many nations viable. Also, a proud president and his party were driven from office.

In other words, the Cold War has failed catastrophically and dismally. Recently Alistair Cooke, one of America's best friends, wrote in the *Manchester Guardian:* "There has never been a time when so many Americans despaired of their own past and present. Only America has suffered the traumatic disillusion in ten short years, of losing its status as the beneficent leader of the world and turning into a giant, writhing in its own coils, suspect, frightened, leaderless."[17]

Obsessive Anti-Communism. Dr. Jerome Wiesner, provost of M.I.T., puts it another way, saying: "Anti-Communism has been so virulent in the United States that it will almost certainly one day be viewed as a mental disease which led the United States to many destructive acts."[18] Even now Princeton history professor Eric F. Goldman wonders if many of our leaders may not be "continuing to think in terms of a cold war between Communism and the West,"[19] and a younger scholar at the University of Victoria warns that "unless the whole pattern of containment is re-examined officially and modified greatly, the United States will be doomed to suffer more, and perhaps more serious foreign policy defeats."[20]

[17] Quoted by Tristram Coffin in *Vista,* March-April 1970, p. 51.
[18] *Ibid.,* p. 53.
[19] The New York Times *Book Review,* January 25, 1970, p. 8.
[20] Richard J. Powers, "Containment: From Greece to Vietnam and Back," *The Western Political Quarterly,* December 1969, p. 859.

Alas, too, the Cold War has been the vehicle for building here the most gigantic military power of all time. As Joseph C. Harsch said in *The Christian Science Monitor* recently: "'International communism', and the theory of a 'Sino-Soviet' bloc capable of coordinating its malevolent energies toward the destruction of the United States, have been the rationale and the justification for making the United States the greatest military power in the world and for using that power in one foray after another in every segment of the world."[21]

It will require a long and desperate struggle on our part to trim this gargantuan military machine down to some reasonable size, but our future will depend on doing it. As Michael Parenti says in his arresting book *The Anti-Communist Impulse*, anti-Communist militarism has "brought us armament races, nuclear terror, the strengthening of oppressive autocracies, counter-revolutionary reactionism, the death and maiming of American boys, and the slaughter of far-off unoffending peoples."[22]

Fortunately, there is a dawning recognition that both the Soviet Union and China must be conceded safety from American encirclement close up to their borders, and that there is no future for any people on earth unless the three giant powers put aside their obsessions and make peace. Fortunately, too, there is now a growing recognition among us that the Soviet Union never intended to take over Western Europe by force and that China has no intention of devouring her neighbors.[23] Even President Nixon now says that the "dream of international communism has disintegrated" and he is moving

21 February 21, 1970.
22 Michael Parenti, *The Anti-Communist Impulse*, New York, 1969, pp. 8–9.
23 *Ibid.*, pp. 168, 175, 189–90.

toward negotiations with both the Soviet Union and China. We need peace and friendship with both, and when antagonism between them is so strong that reputable authorities fear that they will touch off the final world war we must do what we can to prevent that.

World Community. In striving to forestall the final world war it is imperative to remember that the world has become a community for the purposes of destruction and must become one for keeping the peace. Enough world law to take the weapons of destruction out of the hands of national governments is the goal we must work toward, in the not very long run. In the United Nations we have an organization which could be developed into an institution strong enough to save the peoples from nuclear extermination, or whatever more effective death for the world is devised next, if we will rally together in the United Nations in time.

Will we do so? By past experience we will not. We will blunder into just one more world war. Yet man has finally outsmarted himself. He has perfected the means of destroying his brothers to such an extent that if he uses them he himself will cease to exist. Now he has no choice but to grow up rapidly and learn, on the international level, to practice cooperation instead of conflict. He can no longer make the law of the jungle work among the nations.

Biologist George Wald was eternally right in his now world-famous address of March 4, 1969, when in a magnificent burst of candor he said: "The thought that we're in competition with Russians or Chinese is all a mistake, and trivial." A few minutes before he had said: "We've got to get rid of those atomic weapons here and everywhere. We cannot live with them," and of course he was motivated by the knowledge that man is on the way to polluting his environment fatally and to suffocating himself with overpopulation, perhaps within decades. Beside these perils, which menace the life of every people, all attempts to keep the Chinese quarantined are indeed trivial.

Yet our future will remain precarious until an organized world community is established, to grapple with the multiple threats to the continued existence of humanity itself. Of course we are not ready for that, but we are already very late in creating a functioning world community.[24]

The basic question before us is whether we can move fast enough to build such a community, before we "cease to exist." The threats to man's future are so imminent that real progress must be made each year in turning the United Nations into a place of cooperation and constructive achievement, moving rapidly toward dependable world law and administration.

To say that this is utopian or idealistic, after the abysmal tragedies of the two world wars, and after a thermonuclear arms race, the pollution menace, and the population explosion are all well along, is to invite the oblivion which now hovers over us.

[24] Leo Szilard, "Disarmament and Peace," *Bulletin of the Atomic Scientists,* October 1955, p. 307.

II. CAN WE AVERT THE EXTINCTION OF MAN?
Are Environmental Destruction and Overpopulation Controllable?

The history of man is the story of the rise and fall of successive civilizations, some of which left few traces while others bequeathed us magnificent ruins and enduring monuments.

This is the immemorial story of man, but always some other tribes have been able to struggle up and build new civilizations, some of which lasted many centuries. The glory that was Rome endured a long time and a flicker of the freedom-loving spirit of ancient Greece is now being repressed by American-supported military rule. But lately the wheels of history have turned with increasing speed, until they now threaten the continued existence of all men on earth. For the first time we are compelled to envisage the end of history itself.

THREE EXPLOSIVE FORCES

This is due to the convergence of three mighty forces: the ever greater ability of almighty sovereign nation states to destroy each other; the constant escalation of the technological revolution; and a relentless population explosion.

Nuclear Extinction? The first of these great forces is well understood. All really literate people now know that just one more world war is almost certain to begin with the fiery death of several hundred million people and continue until the Northern Hemisphere is a smoking waste. We are so well defended by nuclear missiles in the bowels of the earth and under the sea that we can count confidently on the hellish bombardments to continue until the radioactive fallout in the air kills all life on earth. Don't let the military-industrial complex (MIC) tell you, either, that if we dig vast shelters deep in the earth, and if we have time to tumble into them, we can emerge afterward into anything else than deadly contaminated waste and air. We are now running the last arms race that will ever be run. If we permit it to go on to its usual end, there will never be another.

The Technological Explosion. In the last two or three years there has been a sudden realization that man—especially American man—is raping and polluting our environment in a disastrous fashion. We now see that technology of every kind has gone out of control and that its products and by-products are well on the way to destroying our little spaceship's limited supplies of everything—fuels, minerals, soils; lakes and streams, even water to drink and air to breathe. The old ethic of unlimited growth is about to ruin our small planet.

Let us catalogue some of the damage: First there is the automobile, that wonderful means of going nearly everywhere and doing the work of the world. But it soon wears out, the quicker the better for profit's sake. The hideous car graveyards cover more and more of the earth and each year a larger number of millions of new cars roll off the assembly lines. They must also have places on which to stand and run. They literally threaten to choke our cities to death. One investigating senator has recently concluded that we face "cataclysmic consequences," unless other forms of mass transportation are provided quickly. But can we do without two cars in every garage, and maybe three? Not while the deluge of new cars pours out of Detroit. We pave over the land madly, killing the green things that make oxygen, and there are never enough roads. We now have 105 million cars. Where do we put the next 100 million?

The cars, too, provide the bulk of the health-destroying smogs that hang over our cities, threatening to pollute the air for all men everywhere. It is starkly apparent that the torrents of new cars cannot be permitted to cover the land indefinitely, yet the power of the auto industry is very great. Robert Bendiner, of the *New York Times*, reported, on August 25, 1970, that "Detroit turns out new cars at the rate of 22,000 a day and hopes to reach 41,000 a day by the end of the decade"—a suicidal goal when we already have "105,000,000 motor vehicles burning inefficiently and dangerously some 82 billions of gasoline a year."

Obviously this pyramiding of profits, population, and poison in the air cannot go on without bringing us to extinction. We can survive only by stabilizing nearly everything in quantity and then striving to improve quality. Following the ethic of constant growth much further means very painful destruction for all.

Equally urgent is the poisoning of our waters which takes place daily. Human and industrial sewage have already made Lake Erie a huge chemical tank, all the way to the bottom, in which no form of life can live, and all of our other lakes are in line for similar treatment. Likewise our rivers are used as sewage ditches by the cities, and pesticides from the farms seep into them. These chemical sewers then empty into the oceans, where they kill or sicken tiny organisms that manufacture oxygen. These little diatoms create 70 per cent of all the world's oxygen.

This is a deadly serious matter, since on land we are intent on destroying the trees and other green things which also produce oxygen. Cornell biologist Lamont C. Cole is authority for the estimate that the United States uses daily 40 per cent more oxygen than is produced within its borders. He warns also that the world oxygen supply is both limited and menaced by the fresh inroads of industrialization and more people everywhere. More than 3,000 man-made chemicals have already been identified in the air and even the amount of gasoline lead deposited on the North Polar snows has lately increased by 300 per cent. Lead poisoning kills people slowly.

In January 1969, Russian and American meteorologists jointly announced that the world is now girdled by a cloud of death—our accumulated smogs—that thickens more rapidly each year. Fifty years from now it will be four times as deep. Bob Hunter, an unusually perceptive columnist, warns that we are now at the brink of extinction and that unless we bestir ourselves "the chances are that your grandchild will never be born." He warns that with "the atmosphere slipping toward a collapse" we must accept change with great rapidity.[1]

At the same time, our agricultural technology has broken nature's chain of life by cooping up the cows and hogs and chickens in feed lots and barns, thus preventing

[1] Vancouver *Sun*, June 2, 13, 1969.

the natural manuring of the soil. It has also created big machines of all kinds that have doomed the farmers themselves. They have had to flee to the cities to exist in most unnatural conditions.

Is it 80 per cent of the Americans who now live in cities, or do we have to wait a little for that figure? No matter, the cities are becoming unlivable, as one publisher in New York said to me lately. Their vast decaying hearts are choked with many millions of the hopeless poor, living on relief, while the more fortunate whites flee, first to the suburbs and then beyond, to escape the few blacks or browns who are able to follow them. New York City is now spoken of as ungovernable and near bankruptcy. Yet vast quantities of ordinary garbage— hard and soft, clean and putrid—have to be hauled out of it daily—and from all our cities. Unless better means of disposing of it are invented soon, the cities may be smothered in their own effluvia. How vast will our garbage dumps be even fifty years from now? The beleaguered city of West Berlin is filling its parks with old cars, furniture, etc., and building mountain ranges of hard garbage that will never grass over.

It must be obvious that life in our huge ghetto cities is unnatural and cannot last. If we can hardly shove our garbage out from underfoot now, what will our cities be like with another 100 million people crowded into them? Man not only destroys nature, but he pollutes what is left.

As he multiplies, also, he demands more and more power plants. This means pollution of several kinds. Huge power plants, belching smog from coal or oil fuels, are needed to generate electricity. Atomic power plants are smokeless, but they raise by 20 degrees the heat of great quantities of water required for cooling, and more of these plants will upset the ecology of our rivers. Atomic plants also leave a little radioactivity in the water and there is risk of bad accidents. Also, if they resort to air cooling of their hot waters they will change the climate itself. The great Columbia River in our North West is already radioactively "hot," and "Waste from atomic furnaces, with a danger factor of 600 years, has been found leaking from storage containers only 20 years after being buried." Lord Ritchie-Calder reports that "It is calculated that by the year 2000, the number of six-ton nuclear 'hearses' in transit to 'burial grounds' at any given time on the highways of the United States will be well over 3000. . . ."[2]

It should be clear that we cannot go on multiplying power plants, of both kinds, without making pollution problems more and more insoluble.

The Population Explosion. The constant increase in the number of people also points strongly in the direction of shortening man's time on earth. Few doubt that the mushrooming of people in places like India and Latin America means dire trouble. Nearly all of the population experts predict famines of global proportions in twenty or thirty years, with the next doubling of population, and each doubling takes place faster and faster. It is argued occasionally that we Americans have land enough for many more people, but the weight of authority replies that we

[2] Editorial, *The Province*, Vancouver, B.C., April 22, 1969. One tributary river of Lake Erie periodically bursts into flames from the chemicals in it.—Washington *Evening Sun*, April 18, 1969.

Lord Ritchie-Calder, "Mortgaging the Old Homestead," *Foreign Affairs*, January 1970, p. 211. We are also adding 6 billion tons of carbon to the air annually, which melts the polar ice caps and threatens to heat up the world climate drastically (p. 215).

are already overpopulated for long-term living and that our current population level must be *reduced*. Certainly no one could deny, either, that the quality of life for much of humanity is already at a sad level. It is for at least a fourth of our people living in rural and urban slums.

Moreover, all additions to our population mean more mountains of things to be produced and junked, more pollution of every kind.

Let Technology Save Us. As a last resort many argue that technology can fix everything, if we will only continue our faith in it. Undoubtedly, too, technology can reclaim many junked materials, even at a profit, but the accompanying assumption is that it can also still continue its ever upward spiral of making ever greater quantities of new gadgets. There is no doubt whatever that our military scientists can continue the discovery of new and more incredible gadgets of destruction. To them the sky is no limit whatever. They can always think up something more deadly and more expensive. So too can other technologists. Unfortunately, also, as *Time* magazine observed lately, "The result of massive production is massive filth."[3]

Also, industrial filth in the air promises to end humanity. The same article quotes ecologist Kenneth Watt as saying that with the present content of nitrogen oxide in the air "it's only a matter of time until light will be filtered out of the atmosphere and none of our land will be usable." Many other ecologists think that the increasing particles in the air are reflecting sunlight from the earth. They say that 31 per cent of the world's surface is

[3] *Time*, February 2, 1970, pp. 56–63.

already covered by low clouds and that increasing this cover to 36 per cent would drop the temperature about 4 degrees Centigrade, enough to start the return of a new ice age.

Some scientists think that the effect will be to warm up the earth, melting the ice caps and drowning the world's coastal cities.[4] In any event, the new super jet planes will add hugely to the water vapor in the air, as well as causing damage to our ears.

David M. Gates, director of the St. Louis Botanical Gardens, says that if there were not enough oxygen in the air to filter out the ultraviolet rays, the sun would destroy life on earth; and he warns that "Our continued rape of the natural environment" can produce "an earth populated by half-starved, depressed billions, gasping in air depleted of oxygen and laden with pollutants, thirsting for thickened and blighted water."[5]

How Much Time Do We Have Left? Barry Commoner, sometimes called our leading ecologist, says that "If we are to avoid catastrophe in the 1970s we must begin the vast process of correcting the fundamental incompatibilities of major technologies with the ecosystem. *We have a single decade.*" Other authorities tend to think that we may have until the end of the century—maybe thirty years. The longest estimated lease on life for us that I have encountered is two hundred years. All the evidence indicates that humanity, led by the Americans, is riding swiftly toward its doom, and that whatever can be done must be done quickly.

[4] *Ibid.*, pp. 59–61.
[5] Robert W. Stock, "Saving the World the Ecologist's Way," The New York Times *Magazine*, October 5, 1969, pp. 33 ff.

New Objectives. Surely the most drastic kind of re-thinking and action is imperative and the direction both must take is clear. After working on a Connecticut ecology committee for a few months, John Fischer, a well-known editor of *Harper's Magazine*, found that his most cherished convictions had deserted him. Most of our institutions of government, he says, "and even the American Way of Life are no damned good. In their present forms, at least, they will have to go. Either that or everybody goes—and sooner than we think."

The American Way of Life, he says, is in essence a belief in growth—perpetual, ever increasing growth, I would add. Now Fischer sees that "a zooming Gross National Product leads not to salvation, but to suicide. So does a continuing growth in population, highway mileage, kilowatts, plane travel, steel tonnage, or anything else."

Therefore, our prime national goal, Fischer continues, "should be to reach a Zero Growth Rate as soon as possible"—in everything. "That is the only hope of attaining a stable ecology." Also, his final apostasy from the American creed is "loss of faith in private property." Otherwise, how can we stop the loss of a million acres of farm and forest land each year to highways, airports, reservoirs, and real estate developments?

To reverse the American Way of Life obviously requires quick and drastic political action, "radical enough," says Fischer, "to change the whole structure of government, the economy and our national goals."

These are traumatic conclusions, but they are also plain common sense. Only the most drastic reversal can prevent us from precipitating the end of all history soon. To accept the end of the American dream will be most painful, but consider the following quotation:

"But the dream has become a nightmare. A runaway

technology, whose only law is profit, has for decades corrupted our air, ravished our soil, denuded our forests,
and polluted our water resources. The result is an environment assailed by noxious doses of fumes, sewage,
smoke, noise, filth, chemicals, ugliness, and urban decay.
And the crisis is compounded by a steadily rising population in defiance of all sense and science."[6]

This statement was not made by some agitated professor; it came from a recent editorial in *The Wall Street
Journal.* It is evidence that there must be a quick about-
face if we are to save ourselves from destruction by a
profit-driven, runaway technology. This means a fast-
moving New Politics in which people from the top to the
bottom of our society must join—the young people in
order to live out their lives; their elders in behalf of the
young and the unborn; all patriots who don't want to see
our civilization be a miserable flash in the pan.

Our American Responsibility. We must act quickly and
strongly because we are most responsible for the threatened ecological death of the earth. Though only 7 per
cent of the world's population, we use about 50 per cent
of its resources. In this sense we are the world's greatest
imperialists, whether we like the word or not. Our in-
credibly vast and expensive military machine, with thousands of bases scattered all around the world, is also not
entirely the result of our anti-Communist obsession; it is
very considerably due to the desire to protect and extend
our investments around the globe and to assure the continued flow of great tidal waves of raw materials into

[6] From the Prologue of a landmark issue of *The Progressive,* April 1970,
devoted entirely to "The Crisis of Survival." It contains fifteen articles
on the ecology crisis by leading authorities, including Barry Commoner,
Ralph Nader, George Wald, and Senator Gaylord Nelson.

the United States. This leads us to build huge planes and ships with which to prevent revolution anywhere in the so-called free world. There must be no leftist governments that would interfere with the constant expansion of our investments overseas. If they were curtailed where would our great corporations invest their very large profits? For them the earth itself is the only limit to their expansion. This is the American Way.

Consequently we are the world's great polluter. Our very consumption of half of its wealth involves that. "Each U.S. citizen," says René Dubos, "uses more of the world's natural resources than any other human being and destroys them more rapidly," and, he continues, "our destructive impact on the physical, biological and human environment is enormously magnified by the variety of gadgets and by the amount of energy" at our disposal.[7] We are the chief creators of the world-girdling belts of smogs and vapors, which may end humanity in any one of several ways. So, if the battle for world survival is to be won it must be won here first, or at least concurrently with successful action elsewhere.

WHAT CAN WE DO NOW?

The struggle for a Zero Growth Rate inside the United States will be the greatest in our history. The education of our people to its imperative necessity; the reversal in the American creed of perpetual growth; the creation of new institutions of government; the reduction of the vast power of our corporations—these are crucial battles that

[7] René Dubos, *The Environmental Handbook*, Garrett de Bell, Editor, New York, 1970, pp. 29–30.

will require time, and it may well be that we do not have time enough. But we must enlist in the campaign to create a stable life here, before we all perish miserably by war, famine, or suffocation.

The first requisite is a clear, simple principle around which we all can rally. There must be a fundamental reversal of the conventional belief that those who would stop "progress" must prove their case. *From here on the burden of proof must rest on those who would change or endanger the environment.* This must be the guide to all action. The terms of the game of life have been reversed. We must all learn quickly, in the words of Governor Francis Sargent of Massachusetts in reviewing *Since Silent Spring:* "Blind pursuit of economic self-interest can be disastrous."[8]

While the main struggle is being waged, there are, of course, many things which can be done. Let us enumerate some.

1. Ralph Nader's List:

(a) Establish mandatory pollution standards to be vigorously enforced and supported by penalties.

(b) Severe penalties can include revoking charters of corporations and more severe criminal penalties.

(c) Requirements for full disclosure of pollution by a corporation in its annual report and otherwise.

(d) Require corporate investment in research and development of pollution controls.

(e) Establish new corporation constitutions forbidding reprisals against employees who speak out about corporate pollution.

(f) Stockholders must organize to exert pressure for pollution reform.

[8] The New York Times *Book Review*, March 1, 1970.

(g) Labor unions and insurance companies can exert anti-pollution pressures.

(h) Environmental lawsuits. The courts must recognize that "the *forced* consumption of pollutants by 200,-000,000 Americans creates a new set of enforceable legal rights."

2. Turn our national energies, and many billions of public money, away from promoting the motor and aviation industries into fostering mass transportation by the railways and suburban steam lines. This is a must, if auto smog is to be reduced. This should mean the closing of city centers to cars, or at least the requirement that they be small. The little ones burn less gas and can move faster, thus making less smog.

3. Compel the rapid phasing out of all internal-combustion engines for cars. This means crash action in Detroit and again help from the public treasury. Steam cars may be slower, and they will still keep the oil empire in business by burning kerosene.

Unless the smog cars are eliminated, everyone on this continent may have to wear smog helmets in ten or fifteen years.[9]

4. Divert many billions each year from the lush expenditures of the military and space industries on military and space miracles that will be trivial and irrelevant as pollution increases. Of what use is a vehicle to visit Mars if there is no one left to man space platform earth?

This is an absolute must. We cannot hope to save spaceship earth and spend some 80 billions each year on military and space boondoggling. Incidentally, too, we require some of this money to eradicate the shameful

[9] Ellis Levin, "Smog Cars and the Auto-Oil Complex," *ADA World*, February 1970, pp. 1–4M.

poverty in our midst and to save our dying cities from collapse and disintegration. We must choose.

We should be constantly aware, too, that our government is continuing vast military expenditures, while conceding small ones for environmental salvation.

5. Abolish the superplanes that if allowed to fly and multiply could provide the addition to air pollution that would tip us over the edge beyond which there is no return. This is a health-shattering example of the kind of monstrous gadgets that must lead on to the early end of civilization. If we submit to the superplanes we may be certain that even greater leaps toward environmental doom will swiftly follow.

6. All of our vaunted technological prowess must be concentrated on *recycling* as many things as possible, including water, sewage, paper, and containers. The aluminum beer can is a shining target for oblivion, since it requires power to make it and lasts forever. Other containers must be made of things that disintegrate fast and the goal must be to return everything possible to the soil, to be recycled by nature. The word "recycle" should become a national slogan, especially on corporation desks, if we are to hope to attain a stable, lasting life on earth.

7. Local action is also essential. Tennessee, for example, already has an Environmental Council, with 50,000 members, representing 15 organizations. Several departments of Vanderbilt University are also leading strongly. Every community in the land must have its survival organization and the larger ones must have many. Even school children can be organized to learn about pollution and survival and to police for litter.

Yet we shall fail unless the individual citizen is alert and vigorous in influencing others, especially public of-

ficials. The full power of public opinion must be exerted
against the pursuit of gain into early oblivion—and for a
stabilized, non-explosive life that can last.

We must also believe that it can be done, or that at
least man's tenure on earth can be very considerably prolonged. So let us celebrate Earth Day annually with determination, as a day devoted to cutting the American
Way down to something that can endure.

WORLD ACTION IMPERATIVE

But even this is not enough. One more factor is essential to our salvation—united world action. World action
is indispensable to the prevention of the assaults of the
supersonic plane on our humanity and on our prospects
for survival, and it is equally imperative on many other
fronts.

Consider this arresting list of environmental issues
which can only be handled by international organizations: "the rising level of atmospheric carbon dioxide, the
spread of radioactive isotopes [hence the importance of
the test-ban treaty and the nuclear non-proliferation
treaty], the destruction of the ozone layer by rockets
and high altitude aircraft which could lead to a 'frizzling'
effect because it is the ozone layer which screens out the
ultra-violet rays; air pollution crossing national bounda-
ries; noise from international aircraft, the use of satellites
and orbiting laboratories; destruction of the world's treasure houses of monuments and wilderness areas by mass
tourism; the use of pesticides and herbicides whose effects are carried beyond their place of use; overfishing of
the oceans by one or more countries; the extraction of
minerals from sea water and the side effects of such ex-

traction; the installation of military devices on the sea-
bed; leakage from off-shore drilling; the dumping of
wastes into the oceans."[10]

World action is also indispensable on other fronts.
Whole peoples must be educated to the urgency of birth
control, spurred by the knowledge that almost everywhere each doubling of the population will make all of
the afflictions described above more than twice as bad.
The most stringent means of birth control will have to be
enforced, and the engine of taxation used to penalize
more than one or two children in a family. Children must
not be born to die quickly or to live painfully and explosively in multiplying ghettos.

We must make people understand, says Dr. Harry L.
Shapiro, of The American Museum of Natural History in
New York, that "the prospects for survival are very grim"
and that "survival depends on their cooperation."[11]

Our desperate need of organs of world government
now illuminates our blindness in rejecting or downgrad-
ing them to date. When the League of Nations was born
out of World War I, the towering need for a world organization to keep the peace was pitifully and starkly
clear, yet the failure of the League of Nations began in
the U. S. Senate. Without our great power and prestige
behind it the League failed to prevent World War II,
and the world suffered tragically and unnecessarily again.
Then the successors of Roosevelt and Hull thrust the UN
aside and swung all the way over to American control of
the globe and Cold War with communism, Russia, and
China. Now the tragic folly of the Cold War is clearly

[10] Robert Humphries, "The Imperiled Environment," *Vista*, March–
April 1970, p. 23. The UN is calling a Conference on the Human Environment to meet in Stockholm in 1972.

[11] Vancouver *Sun*, June 20, 1969.

apparent, while many nations suffered grave social ills and the environment itself was dangerously violated.

Now we have our very last chance to help the United Nations to save humanity itself. On June 24, 1969, the UN issued a report warning of the "potentially catastrophic effects" of air, water, and soil pollution and called a great conference on the subject to meet in Stockholm in 1972. It will consider "a desperately urgent cause," for, says the *New York Times*, unless the governments of the world address themselves boldly to the overriding questions of the deterioration of our environment, "the process of destruction may well become irreversible."[12]

The governments of the national states have to do the crucial work of swiftly reducing armaments waste, the destruction of our environment, and the population explosion. Yet they cannot succeed without the indispensable aid of strong organizations of world government. With such aid, humanity can look forward to a long tenure on this planet. A short forty years ago world federation was clearly needed for survival; now it is urgently demanded, if man's time on earth is not to be short and his demise agonizingly painful—either way, he leaves the planet.

These are the stakes, and citizens around the globe must take a hand in the decisions for survival. Each one of us must raise his voice strongly against the acts and ideas, the persons and policies which are destructive. Each one of us must be certain, too, that he can do a little, that he does count, and that the destroyers need not prevail. It will take hard work and hard fighting, but we can give many future generations a chance to inherit a fairly stable world civilization.

[12] *New York Times*, June 1, 1969, editorial.

III. WILL MILITARISM DESTROY THE UNITED STATES?
Is the Military-Industrial Complex Manageable?

"A large, inflexible military organization unchecked by strong civilian review can lead only to a self-perpetuating drain on national treasure, a demoralized citizenry, and foreign policies dangerously irrelevant in a world moving rapidly away from traditional forms of war and diplomacy."
—*The Wall Street Journal*, editorial, March 19, 1969.

It is an almost unbelievable fact that the United States has become the greatest military power that has ever existed on earth, and that its military machine not only considers the world to be its province, but incidentally dominates the internal life of the country. It is also a power so vast that it may be impossible ever to curb or reduce it.

As one who grew up in the period of our carefree isolationism before 1914, I should hasten to explain that the great military machines of Europe suddenly clashed in World War I, and that a new weapon, the German submarine, eventually drew us into that war, to defend our rights on the seas and to ward off the domination of all Europe by German militarism.

The devoted efforts of Woodrow Wilson to end such

pitiful tragedies failed. He achieved the League of Nations but we refused to lead it, choosing to practice isolationism again until another German effort to conquer all Europe, while Japan tried to subdue the Far East, brought us into the even more destructive World War II of 1939–45.

Then the new United Nations was pushed aside by the Cold War, with the Truman Doctrine forbidding all future revolutions, lest they might turn Red, and proclaiming the "containment" of both the Soviet Union and communism everywhere. Very soon the encirclement of China with a vast ring of armed power, close up to her shores, was added. Commitments to defend forty-two states in our worldwide chains of alliances were also reinforced by the desire to protect expanding American investments throughout the entire non-Communist world, giving us a police role of global proportions.

THE MILITARY-INDUSTRIAL COMPLEX

Naturally this gigantic undertaking entailed enormous armaments and a huge military establishment. In his farewell address as President, General Eisenhower warned in 1961 that it might come to permeate and control our entire national life, and this has almost happened.

The term "military-industrial complex" no longer describes the immensity of our submission to militarism. To be sure, there is the most intimate tie-up between the great military bureaucracy in the Pentagon and the industrial interests that profit so hugely from the military contracts, but labor union members benefit richly and even the universities get lush research grants from the

military which put many professors aboard the gravy
train that is protected by entrenched committee chairmen in both houses of Congress. Eric Sevareid spoke
accurately of "the suffocating growth of the military-
industrial-academic-labor union-congressional complex."
All of these groups and others enjoy the very loosely
controlled flow of tax money into their hands. Together
they are still a minority of us but a very powerful one.[1]

At the very heart of this giant complex are the men
who have made the armed forces their life work, especially the officers. General David M. Shoup, a former
commandant of the U. S. Marine Corps, has described
unforgettably the "nucleus of aggressive, ambitious pro-
fessional military leaders who are the root of America's
evolving militarism." He notes that there are "over
410,000 commissioned officers on active duty in the four
armed services."

Their lives are relatively tame in peacetime, so that
during 1965 Shoup says all "four services were racing to
build up strength" in Vietnam. It is war, adds Sevareid,
which gives our officers "their promotions, renown and
sense of being usefully alive; no other experience com-
pares with it for the male ego."

These men are carefully selected for ability and even
in peacetime, Shoup writes, "the sheer skill, energy and
dedication of America's military officers make them dom-
inant in almost every government or civic organization
they may inhabit, from the federal Cabinet to the local
PTA."[2]

[1] Eric Sevareid, "American Militarism: What Is It Doing to Us?" *Look*,
August 1969, pp. 14–16. This issue is devoted mainly to the problem of
our militarism. Among other notable articles is one by Thomas Barry,
"The Marine Machine."

[2] General David M. Shoup, "The New American Militarism," *Atlantic
Monthly*, April 1969.

This capacity is reinforced, says Brigadier General Hugh B. Hester (Ret.), by an enormous propaganda budget in the Defense Department which "covers every segment of our society."[3] On April 20, 1970, *The Nation* published a full description of this public relations program of the Pentagon, "The Brass Image" by Derek Shearer, a member of the Institute for Policy Studies in Washington. It is one of the most arresting and deeply disturbing articles I have ever read.

The G.H.Q. of the mighty program is financed by a budget of $3,647,000 and its total expenditure in 1969 was $27,953,000. This money pays for every kind of effort to influence the public—speaker bureaus, seminars in 163 cities, traveling art shows, guest tours, many publications, heavy financing of moving pictures for official use and for the mass media—all designed to arouse patriotic support for "more and more sophisticated weapons systems, for a world wide counter-revolutionary military force—and for all military adventures in the name of anti-communism."

Of course the Defense budget itself is enormous. The one proposed for 1970 adds up to $78,475,047,000 and Rear Admiral Arnold B. True (Ret.) testified accurately before the Senate Armed Services Committee that "The only real threat to our national security is the existence of huge stockpiles of nuclear weapons in the U.S. and the U.S.S.R. and the smaller stockpiles in China." The motivation for maintaining these stockpiles, he adds, is fear, and "as long as these weapons exist, there is no security for the U.S. or the other nations of the world"—a fact never to be forgotten. "Our military establishment itself has grown to such a size that it indicates a national

[3] *U.S. Farm News*, May 1969.

paranoia and it may well be that its continued growth will bring on World War III which it is designed to prevent."[4]

This is a strong statement from a man entitled to make it. It is verified in an arresting address by Senator Mike Mansfield in which he shows a "disparity almost ten to one between federal military expenditures since World War II and the regular budgetary expenditures for education, welfare, health and housing."[5]

"MAD MOMENTUM"

This is obviously the road to national debility and disaster. Yet we are very far advanced on it. Back in September 1967 Defense Secretary McNamara described the "mad momentum" of the missile arms race.[6] In early

[4] For a copy of Admiral True's testimony consult the American Friends Service Committee, 160 North 15th Street, Philadelphia, Pa. 19103. His brief contains a masterly analysis of the Defense budget, showing many places in which great sums could be saved and our safety increased in the process. Examples: a great reduction in the 3,500,000 military personnel, nearly half on foreign soil; eliminating large numbers of foreign bases that would likely be a liability in a major war; striking out the proposed Fast Deployment Logistic Ships (FDLS) and the huge transport planes that would facilitate our policing the world; ending the monstrosity of "$8,305,400,000 for research oriented toward war and less than 1/20 of 1 percent of that amount for research leading to arms control and disarmament."

[5] Congressional Record, May 20, 1969, p. 140. Mansfield describes further how the Vietnam War "has drained off not only money but political energy and leadership, and public receptiveness toward reform." He finds that the war-oriented complex gives livelihood to 10 per cent of our work force, 22,000 major corporate defense contractors, and another 100,000 subcontractors, with defense installations in 363 of the 435 congressional districts.

[6] "Missile Madness," the leading editorial in the *New York Times*, February 16, 1967.

1969 Professor Milton J. Rosenberg, professor of social psychology at the University of Chicago, surveyed our drift toward doomsday very competently. He found it powered by the "essentially paranoid axiom: that one must conceive the worst the opposing power *could* do and then operate on the assumption that, if unchecked, it *will* do it."[7] This is an exact statement of the rule we live by and it *is* paranoid. It leaves no room for humanity, for normal human reactions, or for the desire of all peoples to live in peace and enjoy increasingly the fruits of their labors.

The paranoid axiom is also self-defeating. As McNamara explained in February 1967: "At each successively higher level of expenditure, the ratio of our costs for Damage Limitation to the potential aggressor's costs for Assured Destruction becomes less and less favorable for us." To try to limit our fatalities to about 40 million in a first strike against us "we would have to spend on Damage Limiting programs about four times what the potential aggressor would have to spend on Damage Creating forces"—and, he might have added, we would always have to sleep in the holes in the ground assigned to the most favored of us.

There is a special madness in the policy of always being ready to wage two and a half wars at the same time—a big one in Europe, a big one in Asia, and a smaller one to suppress some rebellion, say in Latin America. This is an almost certain road to national bankruptcy and internal disintegration.

The whole idea of defense by deterrence is equally illusory. Professor B. J. Kirkvliet, of the University of

[7] Milton J. Rosenberg, "Blind Strategy of Missile Defense," *The Nation*, February 10, 1969.

Wisconsin, has surveyed the whole doctrine and has concluded that the deterrence strategy "seems to be only a rational one for insane societies."[8]

This is an accurate statement when one reflects that there is literally no limit to the deterrence game, short of final national disintegration. Our scientists who are well paid to think up "new weapons systems" can be absolutely depended on to pile new and ever more expensive systems on top of each other. There is no limit in the sky, where most of them will operate.

More than ten years ago General of the Army Omar N. Bradley saw clearly the dead-end nature of the road we are on, with its constant peril of a fiery end. In 1957 Bradley said:

> We have defiled our intellect by the creation of such scientific instruments of destruction that we are now in desperate danger of destroying ourselves. Our plight is critical and, with éach effort we have made to relieve it by further scientific advances, we have succeeded only in aggravating our peril. As a result, we are now speeding inexorably toward a day when even the ingenuity of our scientists may be unable to save us from the consequences of a single rash act or a lone reckless hand upon the switch of an uninterceptible missile.[9]

ABM AND MIRV

If you have nuclear missiles capable of crossing half the world it is logical to invent anti-ballistic missiles (ABMs) to "defend" our cities and missile sites, espe-

---

[8] *International Studies Quarterly*, December 1968, pp. 439–40.

[9] John R. Raser, "The Failure of Fail-Safe," *Trans-action*, January 1969, p. 11.

cially since we already have multiple independently targeted (MIRVs) reentry vehicles on our missiles, each of which can scatter several missiles on the target. Naturally this is not good enough, so we plan MIRVs that can think along the way and then at a thousandth of some second fire missiles at several *different* targets, over a large area. This patently requires super-super ABMs and so on into eternity. No one has yet figured out how to counter the missile-firing submarines deep under the sea, but give us triple billions and a new spiral to national oblivion, one way or another, will open. By this route there is no escape from our final fiery end.

Nor can this game go on much longer. Indeed, the MIRV decision may be the last stopping place before doomsday, for two reasons: first because this weapon must be tested often in the sky and nothing can prevent the scientific eyes of our opponents, in earth satellites and otherwise, from seeing the many missiles on the warhead scatter to targets. This will open up "an anti-missile gap in reverse" for both sides. Indeed, "the Department of Defense is openly putting high accuracy on the 8000 additional warheads (on the MIRVs) so that they can be used to attack Soviet land-based missiles."[10]

The never ending race in miracle weapons is also self-defeating, since the new ones make the old ones obsolete.

[10] Jeremy Stone, "How the Arms Race Works," *The Progressive*, June 1969, p. 26. This issue of *The Progressive* is entitled "The Power of the Pentagon." It is devoted entirely to report and comment on a remarkable and hopeful Conference on the Military Budget and National Priorities held in Washington March 28–29, 1969. No one who desires to grapple with the key aspects of our militarism can afford to be without it. Copies are available at $1 for a single copy and in quantities. The conference was initiated by ten senators and representatives. Most of the leading authorities on the arms race were there and they are quoted verbatim in the report.

The advent of the ABMs and MIRVs seems almost certain to make our land-based ICBMs obsolete. There they sit in deep holes in the ground, in their hundreds and thousands, apparently at the mercy of the new weapons, directly or indirectly, especially if fired from hostile submarines. The Chief Scientist of the Center of Naval Analysis, Dr. Frank E. Bothwell, believes that we also must depend on missiles in submarines, for both offensive and defensive purposes. Thus the Army's fantastically expensive collection of buried missiles becomes useless, at the same time that the Navy's giant aircraft carriers seem doomed to the same fate. Of what use is the big flattop against the new missiles and the incredible speeds of the new planes? In a big war they can only wait for destruction, but meanwhile they can be reviewed proudly by the admirals.

If the plunge into the ABM-MIRV desperation cycle is not prevented, there will be no stopping place for several years in the insanity of the arms race.[11]

[11] Dr. Frank E. Bothwell, "Is the ICBM Obsolete?" *Bulletin of the Atomic Scientists,* October 1969, pp. 21–22.

See also an important booklet by George W. Rathjens, "The Future of the Strategic Arms Race: Options for the 1970s," which was reviewed by a distinguished panel and issued by the Carnegie Endowment for International Peace. Single copies 60 cents from the Taplinger Publishing Company, 29 E. 10th St., New York, N.Y. 10003.

The report notes that "the fortunes and influence of the military-industrial complex . . . are dependent on the maintenance of conflict, or at least a high level of tension" (p. 30). Also, the longer we continue the arms race, "the stronger will be the hand, and the longer the tenure, of those elements in Moscow most inimical to the United States" (p. 31).

An article by Franklin A. Long, "Strategic Balance and the ABM," in *The Bulletin of the Atomic Scientists,* December 1968, contains the bone-chilling statement that target accuracy for ICBMs "is probably in the order of one mile at the extreme ranges of 5,000 to 10,000 miles." This does not leave city dwellers, or residents of missile defense areas, much place or time to hide.

Military Socialism

By any objective standard the American people are on the steep incline of militarism, with the deep waters darkened by the ink of many ponderous arms budgets below them. We proceed downward at an increasing pace, also, because the slide is greased by the prodigal use of military socialism.

Welfare socialism, which increases the health, wealth, and productivity of our people, is one thing, but military socialism, which wastes our resources, kills enterprise, and ends in economic sterility, is quite another. The sweet profits and high wages that military spending bring blind many to the fact that the free-flowing military dollars create no new wealth, aside from some "spin-offs" of military research, and thus end in sterility. Equally destructive is the side effect of killing enterprise and initiative along the way. Why work hard or save dollars when contracts are let quietly without bidding, when costs of weapon hardware are allowed to rise several hundred per cent without any penalty to the contractors, all at the expense of taxes; when new military gadgets costing billions prove to be partial or total failures, without any penalties or relief to overburdened taxpayers. This kind of socialism, the negation of all private enterprise, must bring the richest of nations to bankruptcy and disintegration. Up to a certain point military priming of the economic pump may seem as good as any, but its negative fruits must eventually exhaust our economic wells.[12]

[12] Vice-Admiral Hyman G. Rickover says that our government could save 2 billions a year by requiring Defense contractors to use uniform

We cannot be strong by endlessly squandering our wealth on defense, when the deep social needs of our people threaten anarchy in cities and nation alike, needs that will not wait much longer. We were told once that we could afford both unlimited guns and social reforms. Now we know that this is not true. The military costs eat up the social gains, and weaken us daily.

There is only one way that we can be strong and respected in the world, even loved. That is by building here at home such a workable, prosperous, humane society that all the nations will look to us once more as the model at which to aim. Moreover, we could then have resources with which to help some of the weaker peoples.

OTHER LOOMING PERILS

When human pollution of all of our waters, including the oceans, and of our limited supply of air, plus the population explosion, threatens increasingly to end all life on earth, we have no time left for limitless military waste or for phobias about other peoples and their ways of life. With mortal perils like these to face and overcome —*if* we can—the idea that we are in deadly conflict with Russia or China is "trivial," as George Wald has truly said. The word is shocking, but it is accurate.

We can no longer indulge in the fancies of the Cold War: that the nearly exhausted Red bear of 1945 would gobble up Western Europe, and that the victorious Red dragon of 1949 would create havoc in all Asia with its giant tail. Now that Russia and China have been dan-

cost accounting standards, but the Department of Defense is strongly opposed.—*Nashville Tennessean*, April 30, 1970.

gerously near to war, what requires us to defend all mankind against the two, or either of them?

Professor Fred Warner Neal, of the Claremont Graduate School, has recently pointed out that the claim that
the Soviet Union posed "a continuing threat of military
aggression against us" was always contradicted by "Stalin's inward-looking, defensive, and even isolationist"
policies, "yet this assumption about the danger of military
aggression from the Communist states has permeated our
whole social fabric." We also grasped the illusions "that
we could restrain the spread of political doctrine by military means and that revolutions everywhere were
Communist-inspired and thus constituted a danger to the
United States."[13]

VIETNAM FIASCO

These delusions have been exploded by our misad-
venture in Vietnam, and out of this sad experience there
has grown a real hope that our people will curb our militarism.

In Vietnam our military men and their industrial back-
ers have thrown the whole book of military destruction
at a little brown people—save only nuclear fire—and have
been defeated. The giant B-52s have dropped many,
many millions of tons of bombs on the penisula. Our
helicopters have sprayed bullets and napalm, often at
night, over the villages and countryside countless thousands of times. Even the phosphorus bombs which eat
into the bones of a human being have been used. All
kinds of tanks and huge vehicles have thrashed the

[13] "The Power of the Pentagon," *op. cit.*, p. 22.

jungles times without end. The big guns have thundered and the little ones chattered endlessly. Gas of various kinds has been used, on people and animals, plants and trees.

All this and more has been done and yet the little men who, in the main, fight only with what they can carry have stymied the military colossus of all time. Our never ending military effort has divided our nation, brought it to the verge of internal disintegration, driven one President from office and promises to destroy another. It has aroused a large majority of the people of the world against us and destroyed our prestige with most of the others.

It all came about gradually because the President's military advisers endlessly told him that another dose of force would bring "victory." So the great American eagle became lost in the jungles of Vietnam and does not yet know how to escape. Spending nearly 100 billions of dollars and above 40,000 American lives, while wounding for life perhaps 100,000 other Americans; killing several hundred thousands of natives, mostly innocent people of all ages and both sexes; driving some 3 million more from their homes in the villages to the insecurity and squalor of life in the cities and refugee camps—all this has not given us a sure grip on the so-called strategic spot in South Vietnam which China allegedly coveted.

This incredible and horrible military failure should teach us a permanent lesson about the nature of power. We thought it resided in the Pentagon, but we have learned that it really lives in the minds and hearts of a small people who are determined to be independent and free of foreign control. It is a thing of the spirit, mightier than all the American swords that seek to find and pierce it.

PENTAGON RULE CHALLENGED

If this has not yet been fully understood by our people, the enormity of our military and moral defeat has led a strong minority in Congress to really question and oppose the torrents of military money that used to flow through both houses by unanimous votes, or with only one glorious maverick like Senator Morse or Senator Gruening voting nay. Now every military item is to be scrutinized, by new devices yet to be perfected. The greatest commentators on television now unite in reporting daily the failures of the garrison state. More than a few leading newspapers now use their great influence in favor of survival as a civilian state.

All this would have been unthinkable a couple of years ago. Yet this new revulsion may not be strong enough. The Pentagon is the most powerful bureaucracy that ever existed in any land. We fear civilian bureaucracy but have been blind and deaf about the greatest bureaucracy of all, the one which extends from the Pentagon out over the American empire, to the ends of the earth.

CAN CIVILIAN CONTROL BE EFFECTIVE?

The most important issue in our national life is whether civilian control can ever be made effective again. The very able Defense Secretary McNamara took office "with the avowed aim of establishing greater civilian control over the military," but "the harsh fact is that when he left, the military had greater influence over American policy. . . ."

The continuing paramount issue, Richard Goodwin continues, is whether "the Pentagon is to play a fundamental and perhaps mortal role in shaping our national policy, using secret information, building an independent constituency through a vast public relations program, while liberated from the normal restraints of public debate and congressional judgments."[14]

At the best it will be a long, grueling endeavor, one to enlist the best energies of our youth and their elders. Inexperienced civilian teams move into the Pentagon with each new administration and among other tough fortresses they encounter the mighty bastion of secrecy. "The matter is classified. The public must not know. Our national security depends on it!" Yet nearly all information about any question can be obtained by studying the press and other public sources, if people will take the trouble. The need, says former director of the Bureau of the Budget Charles L. Schultze, is for a new joint committee of Congress, properly staffed, and for a multiplicity of independently financed research centers on military affairs in our universities.[15] Behind them must be countless individual citizens who also do their homework on the key issue of our national life, since our survival as a civilian state depends on it.

Until recently, to quote Representative Don Edwards, there has not been "even an effort to have a devil's advocate against the military." He examined "one series of hearings which ran to 3000 pages of testimony from 300 witnesses, 298 of whom worked for the Pentagon or within the military services. The other two represented the National Rifle Association."[16] With powerful drives un-

14 "The Power of the Pentagon," p. 11.
15 *Ibid.*, p. 28.
16 *Ibid.*, p. 48.

der way to *increase* the military budget in many directions after Vietnam, opponents of the garrison state will need all the aids and ideas that can be mustered.

What Ways Out?

What ways are there out of the military morass into which we have partly stumbled and partly blundered deliberately?

1. *Our priorities must be reversed.*

As Sidney Lens has argued, our imperialistic objectives must be abandoned and exactly opposite policies adopted. For example, all military aid to foreign nations should be terminated, since it is used primarily to maintain dictatorships in power that will look kindly on our expanding investments. Economic aid should be continued, but only to promote social change; if it does not help land, labor, educational, and tax reforms, it should be discontinued. In other words, our propping up of the exploitative elites in the underdeveloped world must cease, in the interest of promoting true democracy abroad and of saving it at home.[17]

To really cure our imperialistic urges, Lens proposes the buying up of the overseas American corporations by our government and their orderly transfer to native ownership. This may seem drastic and utopian to some, but is there a surer way to save our own freedom and democracy at home? A giant military machine dedicated to controlling most of the earth for American interests is all too likely to end by suppressing our own liberties and estab-

[17] See Sidney Lens, *The Military Industrial Complex*, Philadelphia, 1970. Especially see Chapter VIII, "An Alternative to Catastrophe."

lishing a military-fascist state here in the United States. Its worldwide operations drive it in that direction, for there is no such thing as guns and butter; the guns will always preclude the butter, leaving more and more Americans in hopeless poverty. As Lens puts it: "Guns create a power elite that denies butter to the poor and oppressed, that refuses to abolish poverty and racism."[18]

Either way you look at it, the despair of our urban ghettos and rural slums makes repression seem to the authoritarian mind to be the only alternative to revolution here in the United States.

2. *We must recognize that there is no longer any military defense.*

The idea that even the greatest "powers" can no longer defend their lands and peoples is deeply shocking, but it is inexorably true. Every unprejudiced person knows it. When the military titans can only die in mutual slaughter involving the sudden death of hundreds of millions, when an accident or a mental aberration in one man may touch off the final deluge of death and when the military acts of a small state may do the same, the very idea of national defense is emptied of meaning. Only artificial fears can keep the arms race going until doomsday, and we must be' mature enough to refuse to let these fears determine our fate.

3. *The core interests of the large nations must be mutually respected.*

It was a highly dangerous act when we mounted missiles in Italy and Turkey aimed at the Soviet Union, but

18 *Ibid.*, p. 160.

it was worse folly when years later the Kremlin tried
secretly to erect missiles on our very doorstep in Cuba.
Yet it is also incredible folly for us to maintain missiles
and giant weapons of every kind in a close-up ring around
China. That is a sure prescription for a disaster that may
involve all mankind.

*4. No "Great Power" can police the world and sup-
press all revolutions in the non-Communist half of it
that threaten capitalism and our investments.*

Vietnam has demonstrated this for all the world to
see, and no number of FDLS ships and giant troop-
carrying planes can ever restore our fancied world hegemony. When the pressures of population, deprivation,
or misrule make men desperate they will revolt, in spite of
the engines of death and huge police vehicles that we
can fabricate. This means that we cannot enforce Pax
Americana even in Latin America.

5. Neutralization must be pushed.

Many areas of the world, small and large, should be
neutralized by the agreement of rival states; and new
federal unions should be created in areas of rivalry, such
as Southeast Asia, Central America—even in the Middle
East.

6. International solutions must be developed rapidly.

This has been the demonstrated, crying need ever since
the end of World War I. After it there has never been
any other way of escape and this has been more clam-
antly clear during the World War II period and through
all the stages of the Cold War. Now time is short, but

the United Nations, the World Court, the World Bank, and other international institutions still live and their use can be expanded rapidly.

The term "world government" may still be repellent to many, but nothing less than strong world agencies, open even to Chinese Reds, can hope to cope with the looming dangers that threaten the extinction of all men. Every kind of governmental group—local, state, national —and all citizen agencies must work constantly, but the coordination and direction of world authority is essential to our survival.

7. *Looming human problems make militarism irrelevant.*

An increasing number of competent authorities warn us that man's ever greater pollution of our land, water, and air threatens his extinction on this planet in the span of a few decades, and that the geometric rise of population must have the same result in the same short time. Like militarism, these forces may already be beyond control, but we must do what we can individually and in all kinds of groups. We cannot accept the conclusion that man is doomed by his own follies.

In the short time that may remain to us as a nation, and as a part of humanity, we must not waste our energies and resources on military socialism. We must be urgently occupied in helping to give mankind a chance at a long tenure on this fragile earth.

8. *We must work rapidly.*

All around the world our children are in revolt. They know well that their fathers and grandfathers have made a dreadful mess of things and they reject the old values:

that profit making is the main motive in life; that God ordained that a few should live richly while many millions live in poverty; or that in other lands the function of youth is to obey Communist bureaucracy.

Here, then, is a fresh reservoir of hope and action. As the young begin to move into positions of power and influence, they may provide the stimulus to action for at least the containment of our desperate problems and then for solutions that will give the peoples a chance to live at peace in civilian societies, over a long term.

But time presses more than ever. This writer and many of his generation have worked steadily since 1918 to persuade our countrymen to accept strong international institutions to keep the peace, beginning with the League of Nations, but without much success.

Now the urgencies are much greater and the time left to us far shorter. The young generations do not have fifty years left in which to labor, and they must have the help of great numbers of their elders, aroused to avert the extinctions—military and environmental—which hover over all of us.[19]

[19] Some of the suggestions above are based on a fine article, "False Concepts in Foreign Policy," by Fred Warner Neal in the June 1969 *Progressive*, pp. 21–24. Other useful sources are: "What the ABM Would Safeguard," by Winthrop Griffith, and "A Biography of the ABM," by R. E. Lapp, The New York Times *Magazine*, May 4, 1969; R. E. Lapp, *The Weapons Culture*, New York, 1968; "The Military-Industrial Complex," *Newsweek*, June 9, 1969; Hans Bethe, "The ABM, China and the Arms Race," *Bulletin of the Atomic Scientists*, May 1969; and Seymour Hersh, "On Uncovering the Great Nerve Gas Coverup," *Ramparts*, June 1969.

IV. CAN WE ESCAPE FROM CONTAINING CHINA?
How Can We Move Toward Making Peace?

Our attempt to contain and confine the largest, oldest, and perhaps the ablest people in the world began in President Truman's decision, matured in the Truman Doctrine on March 12, 1947, that "it must be the policy of the United States to support free peoples who are resisting attempted subjugation by armed minorities or by outside pressure."[1]

Within three years this prescription for forbidding any more internal revolutions anywhere outside the Soviet realm, lest they might be Communist-led, had the largest possible hole knocked in it by the defeat and exile of the Chiang Kai-shek regime in China by the Chinese Communists in 1949. It was beyond the power of the United States to prevent this cataclysmic event, but Truman's political opponents denied this and his own inclinations led him to make an all-out intervention in the Korean civil war in June 1950, which resulted in a stalemate that led to a heavy continuing commitment on our part for the defense of South Korea.

[1] D. F. Fleming, *The Cold War and Its Origins, 1917–1960*, New York, 1961, Vol. I, pp. 441–42.

The Korean War. The assumption is nearly universal
in this country that Stalin pushed the button for the North
Korean attack on South Korea. After searching for twenty
years I have never found any evidence that this was true,
but it is a matter of record that early in 1949 our government laid down a defense perimeter in the Pacific that
did not include Korea or Formosa and that in both cases
the ruling dictators had no future for their ambitions
unless something drastic was done. In South Korea
Syngman Rhee was in dire political trouble and he had
been threatening for a long time to unify Korea by march-
ing north. That he did so, provoking the North Korean
invasion, is one of the strongest probabilities, especially
since Chiang Kai-shek on Formosa also had been left out
of the American defense perimeter and had no future
unless something drastic happened to change Washington's policy. Both Chiang and Rhee were protégés and
close confidants of General Douglas MacArthur, our
commander in chief in the Far East. John Foster Dulles,
Republican adviser to the State Department and fervid
anti-Communist, also had conferences with MacArthur in
Tokyo and with Syngman Rhee in South Korea shortly
before the war broke out, and on June 22 he exuberantly
predicted "positive action" in the Far East. In his carefully documented book *The Hidden History of the
Korean War*, I. F. Stone points to many convincing in-
dications that these four keenly interested and kindred
leaders had strong reason to expect the explosion that
came on June 25, 1950, with the outbreak of the Korean
War.

This event, for which eventuality the North Koreans
had been well prepared by the Russians, forced the almost lightning decision by President Truman and his

advisers to change their whole policy in East Asia, mobilize the United Nations, and make the Cold War truly
global. Certainly the conduct of the Kremlin in the crisis,
especially its strange failure to return from boycotting
the UN Security Council in time to veto UN support of
the United States, indicates that Moscow was caught flat-
footed by the outbreak of the war.[2]

In any event, our decision to conquer North Korea,
after defeating the North Koreans in the south, brought
in China and led to much additional fighting before a
truce was finally achieved on July 27, 1953, after three
years of undeclared war and two years of negotiations.
Then a political conference, in which our allies in Europe
had all expected to join, was made two-sided only. Our
allies had hoped to have a conference in which all of the
trouble spots of Asia would be discussed, but under the
influence of Secretary of State Dulles the views of Rhee
prevailed. To James B. Reston, Rhee was fierce in his
condemnation of those who were "foolish enough to believe" there was any way to settle the Korean question
by peaceful means, or without his being the ruler of
Korea.[3]

As a result of General MacArthur's rash dash to the
Yalu River and of his smashing defeat, the war had become a long-drawn-out agony, in which all of our allies
deplored our leadership and casualties mounted into the
millions. Our own amounted to 27,610 before the escalation and they rose to 144,173 at the war's end. By then
South Korean military casualties had climbed to 1,312,836
and the other side had a larger number. If all civilian
casualties were added, the total approached 5 million,

[2] *Ibid.*, pp. 597–615; I. F. Stone, *The Hidden History of the Korean
War,* New York, 1952.

[3] *New York Times,* July 29, 1953.

with something like 2 million dead.[4] About four fifths of the casualties came after South Korea had been liberated. They were the result of our attempt to unify Korea by force.

Containing China. Preventing any further spread of communism had been an impelling motive for our role in the Korean War, but it resulted in nailing down in South Korea the northern bastion of our containment ring around China. Instead of keeping our defense perimeter away from China, as our government had planned before the war broke out, it was now firmly advanced to China's shores. We made full use of the positions which our victory over Japan in World War II had left us. We controlled Japan for military purposes and we now made her large island, Okinawa, close off the central coast of China, into one of the mightiest fortresses the world has ever seen. We put on it all kinds of troops and weapons, great air power and heavy stores of nuclear bombs, to be followed by many hundreds of nuclear missiles, carefully aimed at everything in China that matters.

A decision to include Formosa and its professed government of China in our defense perimeter, and another to step up aid to the French effort to recover Indo China, set the stage for decision in 1954 and after to take over control of South Vietnam ourselves and make it the powerful southern anchor of our containment of China—all supported by our mighty Seventh Fleet patrolling her shores, and backed by our immense air power.

[4] The American Encyclopedia, p. 387; *Time,* November 13, 1950, p. 23.

VIETNAMESE BASTION

President Roosevelt had been firmly opposed to the return of France to Indo China. He said to Secretary of State Cordell Hull in January 1944 that France had milked the country for a hundred years and that the people of Indo China were entitled to something better than that.[5] After the beginning of the Korean War, President Truman saw the advantages of Western control of the area and following him President Eisenhower, who believed that the raw materials of Vietnam were vital to us, determined, with Secretary of State Dulles, that the French must not give up their effort to reconquer Indo China.

Nine years of increasingly successful resistance by the Vietnamese followed, a struggle which divided and exhausted the French to the point that they were willing to acknowledge defeat and withdraw. To keep them fighting, the Eisenhower administration poured more than 2 billions of arms and economic aid into French hands; and when France and Britain called the Geneva Conference of 1954, to stop the war, Secretary of State Dulles raced to London and Paris to try to prevent the making of peace.

When nine other powers went ahead without him, Dulles organized SEATO as a cover for taking control of South Vietnam as the French withdrew. He then installed Ngo Dinh Diem in Saigon, who became one of the worst tyrants in Vietnamese history. With our aid, he tried to control the peasants by destroying their villages

[5] Ellen J. Hammer, *The Struggle for Indo China*, Stanford, 1954, pp. 42, 44.

and herding them into so-called "strategic hamlets" at night. This aroused a genuine rebellion, one which the North Vietnamese were very slow to aid, even though the Geneva Conference had firmly declared that there is only one Vietnam, not two.

Eventually, the Kennedy administration had to decrease its support of Diem and condone his assassination, shortly before President Kennedy was himself assassinated, under still cloudy circumstances, as he was moving to make peace with the Soviet Union. Kennedy himself said that intervening in a place like Vietnam was like taking one drink, but following the Bay of Pigs fiasco in Cuba he nevertheless took the first drink by sending U. S. Army advisers to the South Vietnamese army.

Johnson's Escalation. President Johnson was not averse to taking many Vietnamese drinks, after getting a false blank check from the Congress during the Tonkin Gulf affair in the summer of 1964 and promising firmly during the campaign of that year that he would not escalate the struggle in Vietnam. After his election he promptly did so, oblivious of the sad fate of our escalation of the Korean War, and when the bombing of North Vietnam did not get results he declared, on April 7, 1965, that "We will not be defeated. We will use our power with wisdom and restraint. But we will use it!"

Two years later, the extremely proud Johnson was defeated and he felt obliged to become a one-term President.

Nixon's "Vietnamization." Now we have President Nixon, who is the most authentic hawk of all of our Presidents who have gambled in Vietnam. As far back as April 16, 1954, while he was Vice-President, Mr. Nixon told the press that if the French gave up in Vietnam "the Administration must face up to the situation and dispatch forces." Announcing a sweeping version of the domino theory, he declared that "This country is the only nation that is politically strong enough at home to take a position that will save Asia."[6]

Some fifteen years later Nixon became President, after our intervention in Vietnam had consumed 100 billions of our treasure, killed or wounded above 200,000 of our best youth, frustrated Johnson's Great Society program for dealing with our internal sickness, divided our people dangerously, and largely destroyed our reputation in the world.

To cope with this sad situation Mr. Nixon declared that he had a plan, which was finally revealed to be the withdrawal of about half of our 500,000 troops in Vietnam, hopefully enough to pacify the American people, and very heavy arming of the troops of Thieu and Ky, our current native dictators, who preside over a veritable cesspool of corruption in Saigon. This is called "Vietnamization," our object being to hold South Vietnam through Thieu and Ky.

Then as dissatisfaction mounted in this country over the slow pace of our withdrawal the President made an address on April 20, 1970, in which he promised another cut of our troops in Vietnam by 150,000 men during the next year, if the enemy behaved properly. As always the address looked both ways, but it convinced so able an analyst as James Reston of the *New York Times* that

[6] James A. Wechsler, *New York Post*, April 28, 1970. Mr. Nixon is one of the oldest devotees of the domino theory, whereby if one country "goes" Communist the red dominoes will clatter against us far and wide. This has not happened yet and it is highly unlikely to do so, but our efforts to master Vietnam or destroy her have caused the dominoes to fall *against* us in Cambodia and Laos, and probably tomorrow in Thailand.

Mr. Nixon appeared to have "imposed his authority as commander-in-chief on his subordinates" and to be "offering to accept a coalition government of existing non-communist and communist organizations" in Vietnam.[7]

Escalation into Cambodia. But as the President spoke on April 20, the news indicated that Cambodia would probably be taken over soon by our opponents and our generals argued that this was the golden moment to smash the underground headquarters of the Vietcong and the North Vietnamese in two small Cambodian areas not very far from Saigon. So, after conferences with a very small group of advisers—with no consultation with the Secretary of Defense, the National Security Council, Senate leaders, or the Cabinet—Mr. Nixon made a new TV address on April 30 in which he defended sending our troops into Cambodia as a rear-guard action designed to protect our withdrawal from South Vietnam. We would forestall massive attacks on our troops and allies. It would not be an invasion. The purpose would be to end the war in Vietnam and to defend the credibility of "the strongest nation in the history of the world." He vowed that "We will not be humiliated. We will not be defeated."[8]

As the World Saw It. Mr. Nixon declared that "We shall avoid a wider war," but before he spoke editors were deciding that a wider war was probably ahead. On

---

[7] *Nashville Tennessean,* April 23, 1970. On April 21, in the same newspaper, Reston asked if we should "let the government take us into an obscene war by stealth, at the cost of over 40,000 American lives, and not be free to criticize its stupidities or even report its blunders?"

[8] *New York Times,* May 1, 1970. See also the important editorial in the *Times* on August 16, 1970.

April 28 the Boston *Globe* noted almost daily hints that "suggest that we are getting deeply and irrevocably involved in Cambodia," and the Philadelphia *Inquirer* warned that "American public opinion has expressed itself vehemently in favor of getting out of this hideous morass in Southeast Asia."

After the President's address, the *New York Times* (on May 2) thought that his objective assured "a prolonged involvement of American troops and their likely entrapment in a quagmire as dangerous as that in South Vietnam"; and the *Nashville Tennessean* (on May 3) greeted our resumed bombing of North Vietnam as "still another astonishing step into the quagmire," fearing that "the nightmare is just beginning." The *New York Post* (on May 1) rejected the defense that the new escalation was only a protective action for our forces in South Vietnam as "a cruel and transparent deception" and the *Post* observed that "There can be no solace for American parents in the knowledge that their sons will now have the chance to die on Cambodian soil." On April 30 *The Wall Street Journal* quoted "a U.S. General with considerable Vietnam experience" as saying: "There is something basically illogical about getting involved in Cambodia when our fundamental policy is to withdraw from neighboring Vietnam."

The *Detroit News* thought that "the risk was worth taking," but *Newsday,* on Long Island, felt that "It is all utterly pointless, a matter of sending more good blood after the good blood we have helped so copiously to waste. There is only one way to save lives. That is to end the war." The *Newark Evening News* doubted the "whole premise" of the undertaking and the *Trenton Times* defined fanaticism as "redoubling your effort when you

have forgotten your aim." The President's decision was
"a great mistake."[9]

The *Arkansas Democrat* likened the Cambodian
plunge to "the sort of chauvinistic, bowl-game approach
in the Vietnam war that Lyndon Johnson took" and
thought that "it runs counter to the attitude of the aver-
age American, who does not care whether we win the
war in Southeast Asia." On the other hand, the *Atlanta
Journal* said the President took the "only honorable
course . . . despite this being an election year." But to
the *Cleveland Plain Dealer* "His maudlin appeal to
patriotism was offensive." We were not threatened by
what the Communists did in Cambodia and our world
position did not depend on fighting there.[10]

Abroad, the editorial reactions were no more encouraging. In France official sources deplored the new American escalation, and in Britain the London *Times* saw the
foray into Cambodia as "one more step into disaster."
The *Times* was incredulous that Mr. Nixon had "learnt
no lessons from the way his predecessors in the White
House got involved in Vietnam." The U.S. military men
seemed to have won again and "this latest extension of
the American involvement offers military justification and
no more." The London *Financial Times* was almost as
harsh. Before the President acted there was widespread
speculation in the British press on what Mr. Nixon would
do about the deteriorating situation in Cambodia. Most
of the papers predicted he would send arms and aid,
but not a single one thought of his reversing American
withdrawal by sending troops.

[9] April 30–May 1, 1970.
[10] May 1, 1970.

Even among our few allies in Asia the response to our new escalation was not flattering. There was an uproar of protest in the South Korean parliament and government sources talked of "the return of our troops from Vietnam . . ." In Australia the *Sydney Daily Mirror* said, "Oh God, not again! The pattern is sickeningly familiar, and we have all suffered our final disillusionment." Even in neutral Indonesia the Foreign Minister said that Cambodia should fight its own battles.[11]

Widened War. In the short run the Cambodian foray was a military success, as the President so often stressed. Several thousand weapons and many tons of rice were found, enough to cause a few months' delay in any new enemy offensive in South Vietnam. Our troops were out of Cambodia on schedule, at the end of June. Also the morale of Saigon's troops had been sharply lifted by being able to lord it over their old enemies, the Cambodians, who in turn killed hundreds of Vietnamese living in Cambodia and threw their bodies into the Mekong River.

On the other hand, the theater of the war had been greatly widened, in areas of Indo China difficult for us to reach except by the self-defeating use of air power. Very soon the reports and photographs of our newsmen in Cambodia portrayed villages destroyed by our airmen, as in Vietnam, and large numbers of villagers joining the Cambodian guerrillas, as they had in Vietnam. "We felt that we were observing the welding together of the local population with the guerrillas," reported Richard Dudman of the *St. Louis Post-Dispatch*.[12]

In Laos, also, 700,000 people have been made refugees

[11] From the *Washington Post*, May 1, 1970.
[12] *Nashville Tennessean*, June 28, 1970.

by the fighting, in which the U.S.A. conducts most of the
air war and spends about 500 million dollars a year in
paying nearly all the bills of the Royal Lao government
and its people.[13]

By this means of winning friends and widening the
areas under our giant wings, the extension of the war
to Thailand is to be expected, a still more difficult area
of operations to handle. As we push our military activities
beneath the southern frontiers of China, a perfect opportunity is created for her to bleed us by supporting,
or participating in, endless guerrilla warfare. It was natural that news of a summer meeting of Southeast Asian
Communist leaders should be released promptly at the
sixty-fifth session of our so-called peace talks with the
North Vietnamese. The meeting was attended by top
leaders of the Vietcong, the NLF, North Vietnam, and
the Pathet Lao of Laos; by Prince Sihanouk of Cambodia
and by Premier Chou En-lai of China. At this meeting
Chou told the assembled officials that "the three fraternal
Indochinese peoples can be sure that in the common
struggle against American imperialism the Chinese people will be forever on their side, and will win the victory
with them."

Before they ignore this solemn warning, and others
that are coming out of Peking and Moscow, Mr. Nixon
and his generals should reflect that China is amply able
to send her own guerrilla-trained troops south in great
numbers and to support them indefinitely. If they do,
our officials can cease their daily pastime of announcing
large body counts of the vanishing enemy. The Chinese
can also leave it to us to start dropping atomic bombs,

[13] From the testimony of our Ambassador, G. McMurtrie Godley, to
the Senate Foreign Relations Committee, July 30, 1970.—Jack Anderson,
Nashville Tennessean, August 2, 1970.

and if we should do so it would be rash to expect that
the Soviets would not honor their alliance with Communist China. We should remember, too, that the pre-
vailing winds would bring the fallout from our nuclear
bombs back across the Pacific to our shores and cities.
ABC's Paul Harvey has a point also in arguing that
"America's 6 percent of the world's mothers cannot pos-
sibly produce enough boy babies to police the planet."[14]

Furthermore, we should be reflecting soberly on the
astonishing fact of our giant ring of armed power all
along China's coasts, some bases and ships stocked heavily with H-bombs. What would we think if China did
this to us, with bases in British Columbia, Hawaii, Cata-
lina Island, and Mexico, along with a vast fleet, just to
restrain our evil impulses? If we persist in maintaining
a stranglehold on China, we must expect her to move to
break it when her supply of nuclear missiles is larger.
Already the Peking *Peoples Daily* has hinted strongly
that China should have a powerful navy and a mighty
fleet, and Cyrus Sulzberger warned us, on July 31, that
"Peking has already fooled the skeptics in many fields of
technology and industrial prowess."

It may be that China will prefer to help us defeat ourselves, in Asia, until social disintegration at home brings
us down and compels us to retreat from containing her.
Pearl S. Buck, one of our best students of Chinese ways,
warns us to try to "fully realize the depth of the conviction the Chinese people have that they are superior to
all other peoples. . . . It must be realized also that they
are in fact a superior people in many if not all ways."
They are also "endlessly patient, although at all times

---

[14] Nick Timmesch, *ibid.*, May 4, 1970.

convinced of their own rightness and wisdom, whatever their government."

She tells us that "Long ago the Chinese people rejected aggressive wars on any large scale as being expensive, impractical and inhumane," but cautions that they have other ways of getting what they want, such as their steady support of the forces of North Vietnam. This kind of warfare is non-aggressive in the modern sense, but "it is penetrative, it is persistent, it is practical and it is shrewd. . . . At a minimum cost they are compelling us to a maximum of expense in money and men."[15]

The Nixon Plan. Now, she might have added, they are in a perfect position to do this also in Cambodia, Laos, and Thailand. Jean Lacouture, a French authority on Southeast Asia, observed lately that the current evolution of the Indo China war is "the fulfillment of Peking's hopes," and another careful French observer, Philippe Devillers, says that in all of Southeast Asia "all anti-American forces are now entirely under Chinese patronage and encouragement. No settlement in the area can be arranged without the approval of Peking"—even including Burma, Malaysia, and Bengal.[16]

[15] *New York Times,* May 30, 1970.

[16] Jean Lacouture, "From the Vietnam War to an Indochina War," *Foreign Affairs,* July 1970, pp. 617–28; Philippe Devillers, "China the Real Winner in Cambodia," *Look,* August 25, 1970, p. 64.

Robert H. Johnson, a member of the Policy Planning Staff in the State Department from 1962 to 1967, estimated in the same issue of *Foreign Affairs* that we will have to accept "what would be at best a communist-leaning government in the South and a strong likelihood of the future reunification of all of Vietnam under communist auspices." *But* such a unified Vietnam is "quite likely to be able to maintain its independence from communist China."—"Vietnamization: Can It Work?" p. 647.

Lacouture shares the same widely held judgment that a strong unified Vietnam is the best bulwark against any Chinese expansion south.

Of course it will be replied that they cannot succeed because Mr. Nixon also has a plan. It has two prongs. The first is to Vietnamize the mercenary Saigon troops to the point that they can keep the Thieu-Ky tyranny in power over the main parts of South Vietnam; the second is to leave a large American force, say 100,000 men, to hold South Vietnam permanently, on the Korean model.

The difficulty with the first part of this plan is that Thieu and Ky are as impossible to deal with as Diem and Rhee were. All of our tyrants develop passions to rule. The current pair both know that the base of popular support under them is very fragile, consisting mainly of landlords, Catholic and army officer refugees from North Vietnam, and some of the beneficiaries of our endless largesse. Their own troops which do not happen to represent these small groups have little to fight for, while their opponents have a lifetime will to fight for their beliefs..

So when President Nixon assumes publicly that the South Vietnamese troops in Cambodia will come out with ours, Vice-President Ky replies publicly: "that's silly . . . I have no deadline. . . . You are in it with us" and ten days later the Pentagon gives him free rein in Cambodia. President Thieu seizes newspapers wholesale when they displease him, jails his political opponents, maintains truly horrible prison conditions—apparently for some of our battle captives, all of which we turn over to him—and vows to "beat to death" all those who call for "immediate peace, in surrender to the Communists." He condemns a suggestion by Secretary of State Rogers that a war settlement might be based on a proportional representation election and overrules President Nixon on trying for a coalition government as a basis for making peace. Condemning the idea as "naïve and stupid," he will "firmly suppress the coalition movement" because it would bring "certain death" to South Vietnam.[17]

Also, Mr. Thanat Khoman, Foreign Minister of Thailand, suggested on July 30 that the United States may be about to suffer a mental breakdown, which will affect Thailand's relations with us. He resented the widespread reaction in this country after the discovery that we have been paying munificent subsidies to the Thais to induce them to send a small contingent of troops to Vietnam.[18]

Corrupted Colony. Accordingly, there can be no peace, since Thieu and Ky will not accept the Vietcong in the government and they in turn will not tolerate either of them. Meanwhile, AP writer Daniel de Luce found it fantastic to see what 30 billion dollars a year buys in Vietnam—a million-dollar bang with each B-52 bombing mission, a foreign trade deficit of 700 million dollars yearly, half a dozen high-sounding giveaway programs, 745 million dollars in commercial imports, cash allotments exceeding 100 million dollars, a feverish war boom in foreign perfumes, liquors, textiles, and watches, while the slums are growing. You could "see the affluent getting rich," everybody scrambling for a piece of the action, with 50 billion dollars for arms alone, according to an executive in the United States defense industry, as compared to 500 million dollars, all told, from Chinese and Soviet arms stockpiles for North Vietnam.

By contrast with the unbelievable crowding and frenetic living in Saigon, with its pitiful prostitution of the children, in so many ways, De Luce found Hanoi half empty, children able to live normally, the national econ-

[17] *Nashville Tennessean*, June 27, July 10, 16, 23, 1970.
[18] *Ibid.*, July 30, 1970.

omy dispersed over the country, ready for continued functioning, at little or no cost to China.[19] But on a televised "Face the Nation" program on July 19 Thieu warned all Americans that "when the United States disengages militarily they have to engage more heavily to help South Vietnam stand on its own feet economically, and this *will take a long time*." He stressed the point. But how much longer can we afford to shovel vast quantities of money and goods of every kind into South Vietnam, while social conditions in our own vast urban centers decline toward explosion or collapse?

Permanent Obligations. We should be conscious also that where wards of this kind are concerned our protection is forever. Under pressure of the Asiatic drain on our resources, our government decided in mid-summer 1970 to recall about a third of our fifty thousand troops on the firing line in South Korea. However, this modest economy measure produced instant protests from Seoul. President Chung Hee Park ignored a concurrent offer of a non-aggression pact with North Korea and urged that our guard not be diminished. A few days later the entire South Korean Cabinet threatened to resign if it were. It wanted nothing to interfere with the streams of American dollars flowing into Seoul.

A South Korean Solution? Nevertheless, may not President Nixon be able gradually to diminish the torrents of our wealth which flow into South Vietnam and establish a permanent hold on it, on the Korean model? The apparent belief that this can still be done, the other arm of the Nixon plan, has been challenged by Frank Baldwin,

[19] *Ibid.,* July 12, 1970.

who served in the U. S. Army in Korea in 1958–59 along
the DMZ, returned to Korea in 1966–67, and is currently
working at the East Asia Institute of Columbia University.[20] He explains that there are simply no favorable
conditions in South Korea for infiltration and guerrilla
war. The land is craggy, the mountains often denuded,
and cold winters defoliate all cover. "There are no im-
penetrable jungles, no mangrove swamps, no dense forests" and the climate is so harsh that guerrilla activity
can only be attempted in the spring and summer. Korea
is also surrounded by water on three sides and the rural
South Koreans "invariably" report North Korean infil-
trations. For these reasons guerrilla activity from the
North has already failed, after many trials.

In startling contrast, the conditions are ideal for
guerrilla movements in all seasons in South Vietnam.
"Tropical rain forests, marshy swamp areas and rugged,
overgrown mountains afford natural havens to rural insurgents." A benign climate allows them to live off the
land year-round. As late as January 1970, North Vietnam
was estimated to be moving ten thousand men and their
supplies into South Vietnam monthly, where they can
operate in cooperation with a rural insurrection against
Saigon of long 'standing. Also, as a result of our operations, the countryside is "full of maimed, dispossessed,
embittered peasants who may be expected to support
local insurgents." Under these conditions the war in Vietnam could go on a very long time.

In Korea Baldwin finds that the status quo may be
maintained by advancing 1 billion dollars in arms, after
spending 44 billion dollars already on our forces there,
plus air support and a continuing obligation to go to war,

[20] *New Republic*, July 18, 1970, "A Korean Solution for Vietnam:
Bad History and Worse Policy."

but "the cruellest deception" of a Korea solution for Vietnam is that anything has been solved. After seventeen years the little Korean peninsula is still "divided into two benighted, unnatural political entities, each dependent upon foreign assistance" and both wasting their scarce resources in a mini-arms race."

To get anything like this kind of "success" in Vietnam would call for incomparably greater and longer expenditures of our blood and treasure, along with our continued slaughter of the natives, the loss of any remnants of respect we may have in the world, and our rapid sinking toward disintegration at home.

Why Vietnam? Aside from false pride, which is a very dangerous national guide, what is it that holds us in Vietnam? So many alleged objectives have been fought for there over the years that hardly any American is sure of what· we are fighting for and few care. Nor can our best friends understand what we are doing in Southeast Asia. Soon after he became Johnson's last Secretary of Defense, Clark Clifford began to be taken aside at NATO meetings by other defense ministers and asked, very confidentially, what our secret motive in Vietnam was. What we are doing there didn't make sense to them.[21]

If it is to demonstrate, once and for all, that guerrilla war cannot succeed, we have already lost that game. If

[21] Clayton Fritchey, *Nashville Tennessean*, July 23, 1970.

In the July 1970 *Annals* of the American Academy of Political and Social Science, former Senator Joseph S. Clark urges us to put our generals and admirals "back on tap instead of on top" and withdraw from the land mass of Asia (p. 37).

In the same issue A. Doak Barnett, a leading authority on East Asia, now at The Brookings Institution, concludes that we will need to retain some bases in the area, but adds that their number "should clearly be reduced" and in general moved further to the rear (p. 81).

it is to hold a very strategic spot on the map of the world, the cost is already prohibitive. If it is to prevent the spread of Chinese communism, that will be determined by its success or failure inside China, beyond the ability of all our great blockades—diplomatic, economic, and military—to prevent.

At the end of 1966 a team of nine Japanese journalists and academic specialists was sent to China by the Tokyo newspaper *Yomiuri Shimbun* to investigate in depth what is going on there. They all spoke Chinese fluently and they looked enough like Chinese to pass readily. They also traveled separately and their reports were very competently edited by Robert Trumbull, the long-term Asiatic expert of the *New York Times,* in a book, *This Is Communist China* (McKay).

CHINA'S CONTRIBUTION

It reveals a nation of 700 million people striving hard and with obvious success toward abolishing hunger and providing decent clothing and housing for all. The investigators were deeply impressed by the low-cost housing developments, the large success of agriculture over that of India and the Philippines, the low level of commodity prices, and the differences from "the abject poverty which had afflicted the laborers of Shanghai in the pre-Communist days" (p. 157). Above all there was a great national determination, with social objectives beyond the making of money (though the capitalists who had originally cooperated with the Communists were still millionaires!). The contrasts with the old famines and miseries of China were astonishing.

If, too, this new way of life continues to succeed in

China, North Korea, and North Vietnam, nothing that we can do will preserve very long the heavy hand of the ancient landlord system over the peasants of Southeast Asia—and beyond. Also, why should we try, in a time of exploding populations and fast-growing miseries in so many underdeveloped lands?

For many years an unusually farsighted and courageous social scientist at the University of Arizona has been urging that we open our eyes and see the impelling necessity of harnessing the skills and methods of communism, along with our own, to help meet the giant human needs that bear down upon us. All cold warriors with an anti-Communist obsession, along with the rest of us, ought to ponder this message of Neal D. Houghton:

> So overwhelming are the immediate social and economic needs of 250,000,000 Latin Americans and 1,250,000,000 Asians—and the predictable needs of the impending 4,000,-000,000 Asians and 1,000,000,000 Latin Americans (come only very few more short decades of time)—as obviously to call for the maximum productive contributions of all the evolving and prospective social orders everywhere. Each of the new ones seeking to serve segments of the vast underdeveloped regions is developing its own technological talent and its own ways of utilizing whatever of "capital equipment" may be available to it—including the sheer muscle power of hundreds of millions of men and women, which has been the major source of energy in all the traditional economies of all history. And I know of no responsible evaluation of the evolving new systems in Russia or China which does not report relatively remarkable progress, in spite of almost indescribably great handicaps and disadvantages.[22]

[22] Neal D. Houghton, "A Case for Essential Abandonment of Basic U.S. Cold War Objectives," *The Western Political Quarterly*, June 1970, p. 403. No other scholar has ever equaled him in the massive nature of

SELF-DEFEAT

Our penchant for waging long-drawn-out Koreas and Vietnams is also disastrously self-defeating, because it promotes the fall of the citadel of democratic capitalism in our own land. In the Southeast Asia peninsula we are looking over the brink, beyond which lies national oblivion. Besides losing our good name in the world, our Vietnam exploits frustrated social reform at home, on half a dozen crucial fronts, to the point where national disintegration and civil conflicts, or a police state, are coming closer every day. We cannot continue to do what is wrong abroad and do what is right at home. Nor can we continue to try to rule by force abroad without doing the same at home. The killing of four anti-war students—two boys and two girls, all honor students—by national guardsmen at Kent State University in Ohio, three days after Mr. Nixon had publicly disparaged student "bums" who were "blowing up the campuses," is an example of the way we are going.

We are headed toward national disintegration as a means of celebrating the two hundredth anniversary of our republic in 1976. Is that what Mr. Nixon wants? Is that what we want? Must we flash out of the pages of history even faster than we came in?

It is painfully and alarmingly true that in spite of our

his supporting scholarship. For example, see this sentence on p. 389: "So long as Washington persists in all-out efforts to preserve the vast mass-poverty areas of the world as essentially an American imperial domain for private capitalistic dominance, we are predictably destined to face a succession of unmanageable, and increasingly dangerous Vietnams."

This seminal sentence is supported by the careful citation of some thirty books looking in this direction.

fancied "power" in the world, we have failed to find a viable role in it. As I have said in another place: In the fifty years of my adult life "we have oscillated violently through almost every possible extreme; from relatively innocent isolation in 1914 into World War I; back into isolation, by will power and rampant money making until 1929, only to be catapulted into World War II; out of it all the way over to building giant rings of containment, of every kind, close around the Soviet Union and China, on the other side of the world, and finally on to the attempt to suppress all rebellion in the non-Communist world and to enforce a *Pax Americana* in it. It is evident from these gyrations that the United States has become a great danger both to the world and to itself."[23]

It is a shocking thing that we must face the prospect that our national life may be short and our end violent.

To avert such a sad denouement we must abandon our world police role and trust mainly to fair dealing and international bodies to protect our interests abroad. We have gravely crippled ourselves in trying to control Southeast Asia. We have about 15 billion dollars of investments in Latin America and we could lose far more than that in one police operation there.

Cold War Collapse. Instead of laboring mightily to nail down in Southeast Asia a southern anchor of our stupendous containment ring around China, we must begin to find ways to escape from that enormous chain around our own necks. The logic of Cold War containment has at last led us into the final, crushing demonstration of the failure of the Cold War itself. At first useful as a vehicle for the rebuilding of devastated Europe after World War

[23] D. F. Fleming, *The Origins and Legacies of World War I*, New York, 1968, p. 338.

II—when the appeal of communism might have become strong to war-stricken people, but also when the Communist parties of Western Europe were cooperating for recovery in its governments—we have gone on to attempt to contain and confine the efforts of the immense Chinese people in their attempts to create their kind of communism, an undertaking obviously beyond our strength.[24]

CAN WE ESCAPE?

Aside from debilitating ourselves, another inevitable result has been that we have gained the bitter hatred of perhaps the proudest people on earth. For thirty years we have prevented them annually from occupying their rightful seats in the United Nations Assembly and Security Council, seats guaranteed to them in the UN Charter. In addition to our great ring of armed power, we have done our best to isolate them. They have had to struggle up from wartime privation toward a position of real power without any helping hand from their former longtime friend.

[24] In a thoughtful article in *Foreign Affairs,* July 1970, Townsend Hoopes, former Deputy Assistant Secretary of Defense, surveys the question: "Why did so many intelligent, experienced and humane men in government fail to grasp the immorality of our intervention in Vietnam and the cancerous division it was producing at home, long after this was instinctively evident to their wives and children?"

His reply, which he amply demonstrates, is that "The trouble and the tragedy have been that the American response to the cold war generated its own momentum." Our anti-communism became so obsessive that it engulfed us in Southeast Asia, an area in which we have no vital interest, which we cannot control and in which we must "wholly terminate our military role" by the end of 1971 at the very latest—on pain of finding ourselves in "the kind of trauma that could quite literally dissolve the bonds of our political union."

Now the *Yomiuri Shimbun* investigators tell us that "Communist China is going all out to teach its people to hate and despise the United States" (p. 252). Since our thrust into Cambodia, too, the Chinese fear that we may make a lunge against them. Franz Schurmann reports that "Prepare for war; prepare for disaster" is now the most widely spoken slogan in China today. He explains that the heart of their "paper tiger" thesis is the belief that we will lash out until we destroy ourselves.[25]

Feeling dangerously beset and long beleaguered by the United States, the Chinese may well be slow now even to take their seats in the UN, when offered, and they may be very troublesome members when they do. We should expect that at first, but for our own salvation it is essential that China be brought into the international community and accepted as a great and indispensable part of it. This will require forbearance, patience, and wisdom on our part, beyond any that we have shown China since 1949, but we must meet the test, since life on this ever shrinking, explosively populated, and rapidly befouled spaceship earth requires it.

The way back to friendship and cooperation with China may be long and painful, but it must be traveled, for our common survival.

China's basic aims, says Sir Robert Scott, a leading British authority on East Asia, have not changed in a hundred years. They are: "unity, self-sufficiency, security." He thinks there is no permanent conflict of interest between China and the U.S.A. and that by discarding "a sterile policy of containment" we would gain greater freedom of maneuver in foreign policy. It is also "clear

---

[25] Franz Schurmann, "China Prepares for War," *Canadian Dimension,* June–July 1970, pp. 33–35. He notes also that since the cultural revolution they are decentralized, ready to survive a nuclear war, as we could not.

that America is seeking to lessen its commitments on the mainland of Asia."[26]

Concurrently three Harvard scholars have discounted heavily our ability to repress internal change in Southeast Asia or elsewhere, for "nothing seems surer than that in some societies internal violence will be necessary for modernization." Indeed our efforts to support "rightist status quo regimes" make the countries affected "more, rather than less, vulnerable to subversion." Finding China's military moves "defensive in character," they suggested that we "reduce the appearance of threat to China by closing down American air bases in Thailand and withdrawing U.S. military personnel now stationed there." Our government has lately made a first move in this direction, thus braving "anguished and determined resistance" among our many government missions in Asia and "virtually all Asia hands in Washington."[27]

Ten Steps Toward Peace. Among our steps toward peace with China, surely these are essential:

1. Yearly support of a resolution in the United Nations Assembly inviting China to take her seats in the UN.
2. Periodic efforts to renew talks with China at Warsaw, the only place where we have tenuous contacts, with a view to establishing regular diplomatic relations.
3. Fairly frequent informal public offers to establish cultural relations with China, such as the exchange of visits by newsmen.
4. Occasional friendly utterances by our leaders.
5. The evacuation of South Vietnam, after a fairly short

[26] Sir Robert Scott, "China, Russia and the United States," *Foreign Affairs,* January 1970, pp. 339–42.

[27] Graham Allison, Ernest May, and Adam Yarmolinsky, "U.S. Military Policy: Limits to Intervention," *Foreign Affairs,* January 1970, pp. 251–52; 256–57.

period during which internationally supervised elections are held.

6. The opening of negotiations looking toward a Korean settlement.
7. The gradual withdrawal of elements in our armed ring of China containment.
8. Negotiations under United Nations auspices for an agreed solution of the question of Formosa's future.
9. The opening of trade relations with China, perhaps gradually.
10. The public support of good relations with China by all kinds of peace-oriented groups.

These objectives are stated only roughly in order of importance. Obviously, many of them need to be pursued simultaneously, and patiently. In dealing with the most patient and enduring people in the world, we are obliged to demonstrate that we also have good reserves of these virtues.

A long, sustained effort to prove ourselves good neighbors to China must of course parallel vigorous efforts to put our house in order at home. Instead of continuing to slide down the steep incline into decay, revolution, or oblivion, we must work constantly to reduce our military and space budgets and to insist on domestic priorities.

"This is the rule on which everything else depends. With our air and waters already dangerously poisoned, other natural resources being remorselessly ravaged, great numbers of rural people living in degradation with little hope, even for the young, many of whom starve slowly and die early; with our cities rapidly decaying, dooming great numbers of our people to the living death of hopeless ghetto life, and entire urban areas becoming unlivable even for the affluent—with our whole system so obviously failing before the world, we have no choice but to insist that our own house be put in order before we even consider imposing our way of life on other peoples who have old and valid ways of living.

"Scandalous and growing failure at home must doom any empire that we can build or seek to maintain abroad."[28] At the same time we must learn, in the words of John Kenneth Galbraith, that "as in the case of Cuba, a country can go Communist without any overpowering damage."[29]

Unless we succeed here at home, we have no real role in the world. If we do succeed at home, many ways to cooperate with other peoples will open up. Then they will regard us with respect and admiration, instead of apprehension and hostility. Our leadership will be desired instead of shunned. Then we can help others to have a better life and to cope with the social perils that beset them.

"This will mean that the real world community can grow, upon which the survival of human life on this planet depends. Which is it to be? Shall we lurch along fitfully into a short and painful future? Or shall we change course and build solidly for a long national life?"[30]

[28] D. F. Fleming, *America's Role in Asia,* New York, 1969, p. 192.

[29] John K. Galbraith, *How to Control the Military,* Garden City, N.Y., 1970. This little book of seventy pages is easy to read, highly sensible, and of the utmost importance. It is vital to understand also that the West Europeans are doing much profitable business with the Communist countries.

[30] D. F. Fleming, *America's Role in Asia,* p. 200.

The Committee for New China Policy has commended President Nixon for the Commerce Department announcement, on December 19, 1969, that subsidiaries of American companies abroad can trade with China in any amount in non-strategic goods; and for the State Department announcement on July 21, 1969, extending the categories of U.S. citizens eligible to travel in China. Americans may also purchase up to a hundred dollars in goods from China.

This new committee is an active and responsible body which deserves support. Its address is: Committee for New China Policy, Room 9L, 777 United Nations Plaza, New York, N.Y. 10017.

V. THE RISE AND FALL OF THE AMERICAN EMPIRE
Can We Learn from History?

The current American crisis arose out of the fear of communism that has haunted us since this ideology first came to power in Russia in 1917. It challenged the most precious of the freedoms which we cherish, the right to accumulate property, which we have believed was the foundation of all the other freedoms.

This is why the Western democracies tried to strangle communism in Russia soon after its birth, and failing this settled down to ostracize and confine it as much as possible, from 1921 to 1934. In 1934 the Soviet Union was admitted to the League of Nations through the initiative of French Foreign Minister Louis Barthou, a rightist leader who saw clearly that only close cooperation between the democratic West and the Red Russians could hold the fascist regimes in Germany and Italy in check and prevent another terrible world war.

Unfortunately for all of us, Barthou was killed, incidental to the assassination of King Alexander of Yugoslavia, and no other French or British leader was able to put ideology on one side to save Europe and avert World War II. Those in power felt that the "free enterprise" denial of the Soviets was so terrible that the up-surging fascist regimes were a lesser evil. To be sure, the fascists were uncomfortable fellows. They muscled their way into seats of wealth and power, relying on the use of force to get what they wanted and extend their sway in the world. Indeed, their acquisitive lusts were limited only by the power they could lay their hands on. Some of the French leaders saw this and at times urged re-sistance, even in alliance with Red Russia, but British Prime Minister Neville Chamberlain sat in the control-ling seat and, like most rightists, he could never bring himself to join with the Soviets to control the fascists until it was too late. The fascists were rough personages, but they had not committed the unpardonable sin.

Therefore, all during the dismal agonies of the ap-peasement period, from the Manchurian affair of 1931–33 onward, London always decided to help the fascists against the smaller democracies. When they attacked the legitimate Spanish Republic, to aid a rightist revolt, Downing Street even called the European governments to London, twenty-seven of them, to fabricate the non-intervention blanket that was held firmly over Spain for three bloody years, after 1936, until the Republic was done to death.

At the Munich Conference in 1938 the appeasers even helped Hitler to tear apart the fine Czecho-Slovak Re-public, a practicing democracy, opening his way toward the Soviet Union in the east. Alliance was accepted with the Soviets in 1941 only to save Britain from apparently imminent defeat in the skies over her, and the great Rus-sian victory over Germany in the Soviet Union did not enable Russia's allies to welcome her as a victor on a big scale.

FROM COOPERATION TO CONTAINMENT

Real accommodation with the Soviets had been planned by Secretary of State Hull and President Roosevelt, but when they were out of power, President Truman was ready to lead the powerful anti-Communist forces in the United States into the close encirclement and "containment" of both communism and the Soviet Union as a great power. All the Americans who had never wanted to fight the fascist powers anyway supported the new undertaking strongly.

Then, promptly and unexpectedly, communism came to power in the immense Chinese realm in 1949 and the Communist menace was suddenly doubled. To give the Truman administration its due, it had drawn back from accepting the logic of the Truman Doctrine in Asia, but the outbreak of the Korean War in June 1950 compelled it to do so. At the same time the myth of the mammoth Communist monolith, controlled by Moscow and dominating every man's life in the "free world," was born, and long after China and Russia had fallen out, and after many varieties of communism contended in East Europe and the Soviet Union itself, this myth still lives in many influential minds.

Because of it, our leaders went on to build up a great military machine, the CIA and other "intelligence" agencies, and all the vast apparatus for defending the non-Communist areas around the world against any further extension of communism.

ECONOMIC EMPIRE

This global mission naturally brought American officials of various kinds into all non-Communist countries,
all believing of course in the virtues of American "free
enterprise" and in its extension abroad. Our corporations
have profited largely from investments in the extractive
industries and sometimes in others, such as public utili-
ties. A few of our companies, especially the United Fruit
Company, have gained great power in small, weak countries.

Everywhere our influence has been exerted in behalf
of conservative or reactionary governments, lest revolution might open the door to communism, as it did in
Cuba. This has put us in opposition to the rising popular
and demographic forces which must have relief from the
rule of wealthy oligarchies. The great force of nationalism has also operated increasingly against what is re-
garded as foreign exploitation.

DEFEAT IN VIETNAM

It is in Vietnam, above all, that our world hegemony
has collided with nationalism. The American empire undoubtedly sought various things in Vietnam, among them
control of a very strategic spot, containment of China as
a power, and prevention of Communist rule in Southeast
Asia. Of these, the latter appears to have been the domi-
nant motive. Vietnamese communism might well be different from any other brand. It would release the
peasants from immemorial landlord rule, but it would

also close the area to American investments, which have burgeoned under our control.

So we have struggled ever since the death of Roosevelt in 1945, who would have forbidden it, to reassert control over the area, especially South Vietnam. All of our succeeding administrations have had a hand in the operation, culminating in Johnson's effort to smother the Vietnamese in their jungles and rice paddies with half a million troops, millions of bomb sorties, the use of tanks, trucks, artillery, defoliants, napalm, and almost every other scientific method of killing, save only the atomic bomb.

Yet our greatest imperial effort has been defeated by little men fighting in their own forests with whatever weapons the Chinese and Russians will make available—at first with hand weapons and then with various "sophisticated" ones.

Our defeat is unbelievable and stupefying. Our conscripted youth have grown so tired of seeking the elusive foe, and of being maimed or killed by his traps and stratagems, that they can no longer be depended on to "search and destroy," and they are quite likely to destroy officers who attempt to drive them on. In other words, our armed forces are disintegrating, while home opinion has long since turned massively against the futile, disgraceful war that has slaughtered nearly a million helpless civilians and driven several millions from their homes into squalid refugee life in the cities.

At the same time, the American people have been divided and their grave internal problems of many kinds have grown so dangerous that some of them may be insoluble. A faltering, confused economy; far too many unemployed; overcrowded courts and overfilled, antiquated prisons; inadequate and overexpensive medical

care; failing schools; bankrupt cities and states; the determination of our black people to rise in the world; rural
slums; and above all, the dangerous congestion of un-
happy and desperate people in the giant ghettos of our
immense cities—all of these social ills cry out for constructive, expensive remedy, but we have squandered
already more than a hundred billions in Vietnam, and
the drain continues.

Of course all the long-drawn-out tragedy in Southeast
Asia, extended into Cambodia and Laos as aids to our
withdrawal, has badly soiled our reputation in every
country in the world, without exception.

It is no wonder that President Nixon, one of the original advocates of sending troops to Vietnam, is determined to bring our troops home before the 1972 election,
leaving just enough to hold the area against Communist
control and to keep corrupt puppet governments in
power. But he has long passed the point at which he
might eat his cake and have it too. If he will not come
clean in Southeast Asia, a leader will have to be found
who will. His fear of losing our prestige ignores the im-
mutable truth that doing what is wrong destroys prestige
and doing what is right creates or restores it. Now it will
take a long period of doing right in the world to restore
our self-shattered prestige in it.

OUR GOD COMPLEX

At a time when it is plain that we have committed
war crimes in Vietnam, by any definition, *The Nation*
issued a strong call on April 12, 1971, not for prison
sentences and executions, but for understanding how
"God-fearing, loyal, patriotic, law-abiding citizens came

to believe that our adversaries were totally vile, unprinci-
pled, wicked, inhuman, brutal, bent on world conquest,
incapable of change or redemption, and so devious and
cruel as to justify similar tactics on our part."

What the public requires, *The Nation* continued, is an
account of the genesis of America's expansionary policies
in the Cold War years. "We need a public demonstration
of how under cover of anti-Communist ideology (as com-
pulsive in its way as Communist ideology), spurred on
by a domestic witch hunt and an economic boom stimu-
lated by heavy military spending, we launched a drive
for world markets, buying the collaboration of corrupt
regimes, plotting the overthrow of others, spending a
trillion dollars on military programs and acting as though
we had been given a mandate to police the universe."

This is an excellent short description of the God complex, American imperialism that grew out of our obsessive
anti-communism.

But now the dream of our world mission and suprem-
acy has been smashed in Vietnam. We are obliged to
come home and work desperately to halt what one perceptive author has called "the runaway acceleration." Alvin Toffler closes his arresting book, *Future Shock*, with
a warning that we must deal quickly with the problems
of "war, ecological incursions, racism, the obscene contrast between rich and poor, the revolt of the young, and
the rise of a potentially deadly mass irrationalism."

From World Power to Weakness.

For the time being, at least, our efforts to manage the
world must be put in abeyance. Not even the Pentagon
would dare to plunge us into another Vietnam soon. Its

plans to ensure our predominance, especially in this hemisphere, looked perfect. We would have giant troop-carrying planes to rain down whole regiments and even divisions of troops, with their light arms at any free-world spot where revolt dared to raise its head. Simultaneously, we would have a fleet of large Fast Deployment Logistic Ships, FDLS for short, each one loaded with the heavy equipment for a division—tanks, artillery, etc.—ready to steam under forced draft to a point near the disturbance, to meet the airborne troops and smack down hard any group which had the temerity to disturb internal order in our world domain.

It is difficult to imagine a more revealing illustration of our imperial mentality. But now a government of young military officers is nationalizing some of our oil properties in Peru and nothing can be done about it. Even worse, a new government has been freely elected in Chile by a socialist coalition which includes the Communist Party, and it is pledged to nationalize our valuable copper mining properties there, along with breaking up the big landed estates and other reforms. Here, surely, is the perfect compulsion for Washington to thunder, for the CIA to move in strongly, and for the Pentagon to hurl its planes, ships, and troops upon this incredible happening in our own specially reserved domain.

NATIONALISM ASCENDANT

But nothing is done. No ground either legal or moral can be found for interfering and an FDLS-type arrogance of power won't do either. We have to reconcile ourselves to some of our Latin neighbors moving to the Left if they wish. They are sovereign states and many of them are chafing under the activities of our economic imperialism. They may be expected to curtail the activities of our corporations in many places.

This is a serious matter for us. Approximately two fifths of the output of our farms, factories, and mines goes into foreign markets. Our investments in the underdeveloped countries also generally earn higher profits than at home. Branch factories are often an outlet for parts from the United States. In 1964 American production abroad was five times our exports. By 1960 our share of the foreign investments of leading capital-exporting countries was 59.1 per cent. In 1967 298 branch banks outside the United States were required to finance our business. Earnings on our foreign investments increased from two billions in 1950 to nearly eight in 1965. At the same time, integration into world markets has the effect of preventing the supplying countries from gaining self-sufficiency. In Latin America, "despite industrialization efforts and the stimulus of two world wars, well over 90 per cent of most countries' total exports consists of agricultural and mineral products."[1]

INTERNAL PRIORITIES IMPERATIVE

Concentrating our priorities and resources heavily upon our internal perils will be essential during the next few years, if we are to survive as a nation. But we cannot succeed unless we can get soon both a President and a Congress who will drastically reduce the power and wealth of our military-industrial complex and the other

[1] Harry Magdoff, *The Age of Imperialism: The Economics of U.S. Foreign Policy*, New York, 1969, pp. 56, 75, 177–78, 197.

giant bureaucracies which are accustomed to lavish tax support.

Seymour Melman, our leading authority on this subject, explains often that pouring out public funds on military gadgets does create some temporary jobs and profits but that the end result is parasitic. Since 1945 we have spent 1100 billion dollars for military purposes, more than "the value of all business and residential structures in the United States." More than half of our technical researchers have been employed on unproductive undertakings, while New York City and others "display the main aspects of an underdeveloped economy."

Whole industries have become technologically and organizationally depleted, including "apartment house construction, ship building, steel and many of the machinery-producing industries. The railroads resemble Toonerville Trolleys. Many military-industrial engineers now have a trained incapacity for civilian work."[2]

CAN WE REDUCE OUR APPARATUS OF EMPIRE?

This points to what could be the fatal result of our Cold War and empire-building mentalities. In an outstanding article in the new quarterly *Foreign Policy*, John K. Galbraith stresses that huge entrenched nonproductive bureaucracies may be our undoing. "Military missions, military advisers, active military formations, counterinsurgency teams, pacification teams, technical assistance teams, advisers on aid utilization, auditors and inspectors . . . , information officers, intelligence officers, spooks—the list extends almost indefinitely."

[2] Seymour Melman, *New York Times*, November 3, 1970.

Where, as in Vietnam and Laos, he continues, "the frustration has been nearly total, the bureaucratic input has been all but infinite." But elsewhere throughout the free world "the sixties saw the deployment of a huge American military, counterinsurgency, intelligence, diplomatic, public information and aid establishment designed to influence potentially erring governments and people away from Communism."[3]

This burden of imperial bureaucracy is a frightening thing. We have a large part of our best talent unproductively employed and bureaucratized to defend sterile ways of life. "The national need can dissolve and become ludicrous as in the case of Vietnam." Galbraith continues, "but this does not affect the need of an army for the occupation, prestige, promotions that go with active military operations; the need of the CIA for the interest, personal drama, excitement, and outlet for money that go with its Laotian adventures; or the need of the Air Force for bombing as a *raison d'être*."

All of the common sense and determination of the American people will be required to reduce gradually these tremendous bureaucratic powers and turn most of the people in them into productive work. Of course we shall require fairly large military expenditures in a world of three great rival powers, but some 10-billion-dollar cuts annually are required. It is shocking that there will be none in 1971, in a time when national disintegration threatens. This goes also for the other great agencies for controlling the world.

We must greatly "contract our policy in Latin America, Africa and Asia. This means specifically that we no longer

[3] *Foreign Policy*, Winter 1970–71, pp. 31–45.

stand guard against what is called Communism in these parts of the world."[4]

The Cold War and its associated American empire building have forced this great people to look over the brink beyond which lies oblivion. Now we must have great efforts of insight and leadership to enable us to rebuild here at home a healthy, civilized society, one that takes care of all of its people and is again worthy of respect and emulation. Once the world did look to us with respect, and it can be so again, but this will not happen unless our people generally rise to the need for rebuilding—before it is too late.

[4] *Ibid.*, p. 43.

VI. CAN WE HALT OUR INTERNAL DECLINE?
Must Our National Life Be Short?

On December 25, 1965, one of the Americans who knows most about Asia published in the *New Republic* this warning to President Johnson, and to all of us. He said:

> The President's problem is to make his people see that it can only be a way *out*, not a way farther into Indo China. Even the United States, with all its military power, wealth and good intentions, does not possess the means unilaterally to impose a durable political decision in territory so remote from its homeland, so removed from its vital interests, in violation of international treaty obligations recognized by its allies and enemies alike, in transgression against the United Nations Charter, and manifestly irreconcilable with the sovereign rights and capabilities of a people innocent of aggression against the United States and determined on independence and national unity. . . .

In other words, Edgar Snow was warning us that with all our military power and wealth we could not impose our way of life on the little peoples of Southeast Asia. How deadly right he was, as everyone can see now.

But in 1965 even Edgar Snow could not foresee that our attempt to control the Vietnamese people, by violating all the international laws that matter, would lead to a debilitation of our own national life so grave as to endanger our future existence as a viable nation.

On November 15, 1970, five years after Snow wrote, the *New York Times* said:

> "American cities are in an aimless drift. The slums not only dehumanize those who live in them but contaminate the physical and economic security of the entire urban area. Transportation and communications are declining, as though their problems were unrelated to the huge untapped potential of innovative planning. Pollution of air and water eats away at the environment, just as the pollution of mind and words corrodes relations between people."—*New York Times*, editorial, November 15, 1970.

Half a year later, on April 25, 1971, the *New York Times* asked, almost in despair, "Can the old cities be saved: Do Americans want to save them?" Listing New York, Newark, Boston, Philadelphia, Baltimore, Cleveland, Detroit, Chicago, and St. Louis as all sliding down the same desperate track, the *Times* pointed out that the urban dilemma is the nation's dilemma, that the cities cannot save themselves, that the situation can only get worse, and that so far the state and national governments refuse to save the cities.

Of course this desperate state of affairs is not due entirely to the follies of the Vietnam War. When Lyndon B. Johnson was elected President of the Great American Republic by a huge landslide vote in November 1964, the need for sweeping social and economic reform was widespread and urgent. In the campaign he had also promised the people that he would not be diverted by involvement in the Vietnam civil war which had been running for many years.

Yet as soon as he could be inaugurated in January he broke that pledge. His generals in their splendor told him how they could use the tremendous firepower at their disposal to crush North Vietnam quickly, and he decided that he could have both victory in Vietnam and the great program of internal reforms to which he was sincerely pledged. He was also able to get his Great Society program enacted into law in the early part of 1965, as the great bombers thundered over Vietnam, hurling their doom on friend and foe alike. The slaughter was terrific and horrible, but it didn't work. With his own pride and that of his generals committed, he soon found that the money for his Great Society reforms was increasingly being siphoned off to Vietnam. Military spending in Vietnam ran up to a peak of 29 billion dollars, while total defense outlays accelerated to 81.2 billion in 1969 and are estimated to be 76.6 billion in 1970. The total direct military cost of the Vietnam War to the end of 1970 came to 106.9 billion, and the indirect, supporting costs may have been almost as large.[1]

Certainly the five war years beginning in January 1965 have seen a great decline in our chances of continuing to

[1] William Lerner, *Pocket Data Book*, U.S.A., 1969, U. S. Department of Commerce.

In addition to the shocking loss of native and American lives, another sad cost of the Vietnam adventure is the destruction of the land. The Stanford Biology Study Group has published a most disturbing booklet, "The Destruction of Indo-China," which details our defoliation and crop destruction, involving starvation as a weapon and birth defects for the native children; forest destruction by fires set and by shrapnel, which by removing nature's cover turn the soil into laterite—a bricklike substance; and bombing that leaves the land a sea of craters 45 feet across and 30 feet deep. For copies write to Box 3724, Stanford, California.

be the Great Republic. It may well be that this half decade has marked the beginning of our permanent decline
as a nation and a civilization. If this is not to be, we must
surely cut drastically, on a long-term basis, the great tide
of military spending that has been moving us toward
disintegration.

IMPERATIVE TASKS

We must also exert ourselves mightily to keep from
being smothered by overurbanization in our decaying
cities; to create a national transportation system that will
enable great numbers of people to ride comfortable,
speedy trains into and between our cities; to rebuild our
shocking slums and much other housing; to rescue our
run-down education system and renovate it from top to
bottom; to reform drastically our whole system of courts
and prisons; to reduce the tensions of racial conflict before they erupt dangerously; to care for our old people
more adequately; to reform our derelict health services;
to provide annual family incomes and employment in
place of the degradation and failure of welfare relief; to
deal with the multiple perils of the pollution of our air,
water, and soils before we are all smothered or poisoned;
to stop the increase in population and give ourselves
stable numbers that can expect to live in decency and
safety, generation after generation. To have a good
chance of doing all this we must break the dead hand of
seniority and senility over our Congress, to free it for the
great, regenerative labors that are required of it, if we
are to halt our decline and become a great, constructive
force in the world, instead of a destructive, declining
giant.

Where to Live? There is something obviously unnatural and temporary in the vast aggregations of people
that we have accumulated in the huge megalopolises
stretching from Boston to Washington, from Chicago to
Buffalo, and in Southern California. Fortunately, plans
are being made to erect whole new cities, even in the
100,000 class, in an effort to stem the piling up of our
people in skyscrapers and slums, but these too will be
ineffective unless our population is stabilized. It must
always be kept in mind that everything will become insoluble unless this goal is achieved.

While we work on this key undertaking, really heroic
efforts must be made to make our big urban areas livable
again. This involves the destruction of many slums and
the building of many new homes for all kinds of people.
The new Master Plan for New York City has declared
that the welfare of the white middle class is vital, and
that this must be remembered while improving the lot
of the poor blacks and Puerto Ricans. This is obviously
true, but decent housing can be provided for all.

Great Britain has proved that it can be done. Ada
Louise Huxtable of the *New York Times* reports that by
1973 there will be a 6 per cent housing surplus in Britain,
or 1 million homes over households. The new houses are
of many types, from small villas to skyscrapers. Some
developments are success dreams; others are high and too
near the tracks. There are all kinds of criticisms, including prospects of moral alienation for many, but the thing
has been done. The houses are there.[2]

Here the task is far greater, as is the continuing danger
of moral alienation. The old people in the great Red Hook
houses of New York City, built in the New Deal period,

[2] *New York Times*, November 16, 1970.

now huddle in their rooms after a murder of one of their number, and the buildings are grimy, with lawns and alleys littered. But the many welfare families now living in hotels find life "horrible," with big families jammed into one or two sparsely furnished rooms.[3]

Mass Transport. While we gird for a great effort to rebuild much of our cities, and to move many people out into new cities, the rescue of the cities from traffic strangulation is urgent and imperative. The daily effort of many millions of suburban residents to go to work in the city in their autos chokes the city streets early in the day, when added to the service traffic that normally flows. Nor is any cure in sight short of building new rapid transit railway systems that will move great numbers of people in and out of the cities quickly and in comfort, while their cars and smog stay at home.

The same efficient railway service is required also between cities in our congested areas and, again, we know that it can be done. The Japanese have proved it by providing super-express service along their megalopolis from Tokyo to Osaka. Clean, comfortable, beautiful cars, running frequently at 125 miles an hour, are filled with satisfied passengers; or one can go on the ordinary express or a local train, moving on separate tracks. While we militarized ourselves, fought the Cold War, and bombed Vietnam, the Japanese, often called imitators, have given their cities one of the requisites of survival. Of course they will have to go further, since oxygen is now sold to pedestrians on Tokyo streets and taxi drivers are taken to oxygen stations to be reconditioned for further driving.

By comparison with Japan's railway achievement, our

[3] *Ibid.*, November 23, 1970.

government has made "a small shaky start" toward saving our train service from oblivion. A new rail corporation is projected in which the government will invest 40 million dollars and guarantee 100 million dollars of loans to railways desiring to invest in the corporation, which is supposed to make a profit. If it does not do so by July 1, 1973, it will be empowered to reduce the already skimpy national network proposed, which, for example, would not provide any service along the populous Pacific coast.

In an outstanding article at the beginning of December 1970, Tom Wicker found "this niggardly approach" in "stark and utterly senseless contrast to the $200 million further investment Congress even now is being asked to make in that unnecessary and uneconomic monument to pollution and technological chauvinism" the giant SST plane, which would carry so few at such huge costs and risks to others. Then he compared the pittance feebly offered for train service to the current authorization by the House of 17.3 billion dollars more to complete the 42,500-mile interstate highway system by 1978. This, said Wicker, "not only represents a staggering level of investment for paving a great deal of the countryside, bulldozing under much of our cities and turning a high proportion of American air blue and noxious; it is also an investment stupendously out of proportion to the low efficiency and poor cost-effectiveness of automobile transportation"—a comparison which suggests that we shall have to exert ourselves mightily to keep from being motorized to death.

Wicker showed that an investment of several hundred million dollars in new roadbed would enable current train technology to provide a train schedule of two hours and fifteen minutes between Boston and New York "that would be competitive with the airlines, beat the automobile on a time basis, and leave both far behind in passenger capacity." At the same time, the big cost of new airports for New York could be avoided, since one fifth of all air passengers come from Boston and Washington, and people would get better and more efficient service. "By every such measure, the case for modern rail passenger service in America is overwhelming."[4]

Modern railway service, including new subways in the place of our antiquated ones that are a daily peril to so many, would also advance the time when many city streets could be closed to auto traffic and given over entirely to the people—at least for some hours of the day—a dream of peace and leisure which foreign cities are already attaining. Why not here?

Alas, the answer is that our leaders prefer to spend many times what it would cost to build a fine system of mass transportation on trips to the moon and outer space. Moreover, this shameful stultification of our degenerating life will continue until we can get governments which will work to prolong man's imperiled tenure on earth.

Ending Endemic Poverty. On the fundamental level of human needs, is it not time for us to support strongly President Nixon's admirable family assistance plan, which the *New York Times* calls "critically important legislation"? A government guarantee of $1600 annually for every family of four is not much, but enough to establish a floor of security, self-respect, and hope which should lead to efforts at self-help to rise a little—if education, health, ability, and opportunity permit. Even if this should not happen, the family assistance stipend can

---

[4] *Nashville Tennessean,* December 2, 1970. A good suburban railway system would also enable people from the ghettos to go to work in the suburbs, where there are many opportunities.

replace most of the present welfare relief that involves so many abuses and so much bureaucracy.

In each of the fifty states "it would be a powerful economic force for holding impoverished families together and for breaking the vicious poverty cycle." Given tolerable success in reducing the astronomical costs of ever more fantastic military-miracle gadgets, the plan can be expanded to give us a fairly decent society. It could even reach into the maze of narrow valleys and nearly inaccessible hollows at the top of Appalachia to aid the poorest in that area, who seem to have been untouched by the great Appalachian aid program which followed President John F. Kennedy's shock at what he saw there on his first visit. Since 1960 there has been some 7 billion dollars in public investment in the thirteen-state Appalachian region, but the director of the Appalachian Regional Commission says: "There are still millions of people in Appalachia who do not have access to a good education, or to decent health, or to an adequate job, and who still live below a level of acceptable income. From their point of view, not very much has been accomplished to date," he concluded, and this is especially true of the million people in the high valleys.

The commission's strategy has been to invest intensively in selected small town areas, hoping that the benefits and examples would spread. It was frankly an application of "trickle-down" economics and it has not worked. "Logrolling politics" spread the efforts made too thinly. Thus entrenched political interests and those already well-to-do have profited, but not the highlanders. Spurred by enormous investment in road building, new factories and jobs have put 150,000 people on payrolls, but even in the lower areas the new highways "pass in many places through a right-of-way of poverty, like urban freeways over a ghetto."[5]

A year later when a *New York Times* reporter accompanied Senator Edward M. Kennedy's Senate Health Subcommittee to Appalachia on April 20, 1971, they heard dozens of. persons tell, "sometimes tearfully, of waiting hours to have broken bones set, of relatives dying without medical attention and of children who had never seen a doctor or a dentist."

Senator Ernest F. Hollings, of South Carolina, also wrote, in the same week, that hunger is a reality for 15 million hard-core poor Americans and that another 10 million stand in need of some food assistance. Hunger, he said, "stalks in every corner of America and haunts citizens of every color—twice as many white as red and black combined. The situation is the more cruel because it is unnecessary" (*The Nation*, April 26, 1971, pp. 518–21).

We can add truthfully that this situation is a shame and disgrace—a telling indictment not only of our profligate Cold War spending but of our economic and governmental systems.

Isn't it high time that we really tried the "trickle-up" propensities of the family assistance plan? Isn't there a strong probability that from Appalachia to Harlem and from Mississippi to Chicago the program would help to rebuild lives, local prosperity, and national self-respect?

Of course, the problem of poverty requires even more drastic measures. A comprehensive report from the prestigious Committee for Economic Development has disclosed that nearly 50 per cent of those locked in urban poverty are "simply not susceptible to being saved from

[5] Ben A. Franklin, "In Appalachia: Vast Aid, Scant Relief," *New York Times*, November 29, 1970.

it without radical and expensive new government programs," and this category of people is multiplying so fast that by 1985 it will be a major population force in our large cities. By that year also poverty-prone non-whites will have absolute majorities in nine of our large cities, named in the report.[6]

Are we really determined to continue spending endless billions on the newest missile, or plane, or space vehicle, while the foundations of our society continue to sink beneath us?

Neglected Schools. While for twenty-five years we have fought something called the Cold War, by building a vast military apparatus to prevent the spread of communism and to assert our power and economic ascendancy around the world, our schools have fallen far behind the needs of the nation. One reason is that large numbers of slum children suffer from lack of food, which makes them mentally retarded for life. But many schools themselves stultify bright minds. A 1970 report commissioned by the Carnegie Corporation found that the public schools throughout the country are too often oppressive, grim, and joyless. They are so preoccupied with order and routine that pupils are "subjugated" by uniform teaching "that tends to destroy students' curiosity along with their ability."[7] On the other hand, many schools and classes are disrupted by violent older pupils.

This is not altogether strange at a time when the first national priority is the application of force and violence for the control of Southeast Asia, and the compulsion of our youth to engage in the undertaking. At the same time, higher education is under heavy financial attack

[6] "Poverty: A Losing War," *Newsweek*, November 23, 1970, p. 117.
[7] *New York Times*, September 20, 1970.

from those who resent the resistance of youth and its quest for new life forms. Our entire system of education, from bottom to top, is under great strain.

Another Carnegie study reported, on December 4, 1970, that our colleges and universities face "the greatest financial crisis" in our history, one which can be overcome only by a massive national effort, involving increased contributions by both the federal and state governments.[8] Our educational system demands great amounts of the attention, ability, and money that are being wasted in Vietnam, if we are to hope to rebuild our national life in a time of rapid change and multiplying problems.

Failing Courts and Prisons. Strong remedial action is also demanded in our entire system of justice. A *Life* correspondent back from Asia, on August 7, 1970, was "astonished at the depths of bitterness, hostility and suspicion" at home and especially at the breakdown of the courts.

After a weekend of rioting in half a dozen New York City prisons in early October, Mayor John Lindsay issued a long statement in which he defended the grievances of the thousands of inmates who rioted. He "described overcrowded jails as inhumane and characterized the court system as tottering on the brink of failure." Lindsay insisted on day and night court sessions until the backlog of criminal cases, estimated at 90,000 to 345,000, was cleared up. He demanded also a drastic overhaul of bail policies, including reduced bails and the offering of cash-bail alternatives to every defendant, and the establishment of time limits on detention before trial.[9]

At the same time, discontent seethed in the New York

[8] *Ibid.*, December 4, 1970.
[9] *Ibid.*, October 11, 1970.

State prison system, generating a heavy file of lawsuits from prisoners which shook the bureaucracy, the routine, and the discipline of the system. Prisoners were much more conscious of their civil rights than ever before and in rebellion against some of the more inhumane punishments. At the Kansas State Penitentiary, more than a hundred years old, three hundred prisoners had slashed their arms and legs, some cutting their Achilles' tendons, in protest against the regulations of a new commissioner and against long neglect. Yet it is possible to find in Texas a progressive penal system in which more than seven thousand prisoners regularly attend school, from the first grade through junior college, and nearly all of the thirteen thousand prisoners are given an opportunity to get an education rather than work in shops or in the fields. The result is that only 18 per cent of the released prisoners are returned for new offenses, as compared with 50 per cent and above elsewhere.[10]

By contrast, the *New York Times* demanded prison facilities that do not degrade and dehumanize the jailed, new bail procedures that do not lump together hardened felons and those confined by the law's delay, and more judges, lawyers, and courtrooms, so that hearings do not have to take place (literally) in cloakrooms.[11] In Nashville, federal judge William E. Miller held that confining a man naked in an empty concrete cell, a common practice in various states, violated a man's constitutional rights.

Virtually all experts, says columnist Joseph Kraft, "stress the crucial importance of improving a penal sys-

[10] *Ibid.*, November 15, December 4; *Nashville Tennessean*, September 8, 1970.
[11] *New York Times*, September 14, October 5, November 19, 1970.

tem which, as now constituted, tends to breed rather than
to scotch crime." This is vital at a time when fear of social
discontent and crime leads to demands for jailing more
people, and when the Congress is passing laws legalizing
forcible entry by police and preventive detention, while
the arsenals of police weapons grow daily.

Yet in his book *Crime in America*, Ramsey Clark, the
most intensely human Attorney General we have ever
had, warns that "Repression is the one clear course toward irreconcilable division and revolution in America."
The police must be better trained and paid, but disarmed.
He believes that wire tapping is more than a dirty business; it tinkers with personal integrity itself. Our bail
system, he holds, discriminates against the poor, and preventive detention is "another cheap and immoral excuse
for failing to meet the needs of modern society." Altogether, says Clark, "Excessive reliance on the system of
criminal justice is terribly dangerous. It separates the
people from their government." There is "no conflict
between liberty and safety. We will have both, or
neither."[12]

Quite obviously we need to give much larger amounts
of attention, concern, and money to rehabilitation of
what one specialist calls "our awful prisons and jails."
Ronald L. Goldfarb tells us that we have about 400 prisons, housing over 300,000 adults and 54,000 juveniles,
and over 5000 jails holding all manner of minor offenders
and unfortunates whom we don't want on the streets. He
finds hope for reform in the fact that many of the best
of the current generation of young people will be ex-
convicts, due to their resistance to war and the draft, to
college rebellions and the drug cult. As these children of

[12] *Ibid.*, November 19, 1970.

the influential classes rise to positions of influence, reforms may be accelerated.[13]

For the short term, the *New Republic* (October 24, 1970) proposes three steps which would reduce the jail population and help restore ex-convicts to productive life: "1. Eliminate most crime-without-victims from our criminal law system: drunk and disorderly conduct, prostitution, drug offenses, and gambling. This would flush countless cases out of courts, so that cases can be given individual attention and delays eliminated. 2. Make it more difficult to give prison sentences for first offenses and develop a wider range of probation services, with adequate manpower and control. 3. Provide funds on a massive scale for decent jobs with a future for all who are placed on probation or parole."

These common-sense rules would help greatly while fundamental reforms of our entire penal system proceed. A great nation that thought it could police the world can and must clean up its own internal police operations. But of course the real remedy is to attack the social and economic conditions that breed crime—excessive crowding of people in too little living space, hopeless poverty and degrading welfare relief, nothing for youth to do (especially blacks) except stand on the streets, slum living alongside great affluence, and hopeless outlooks.

THE CORPORATE STATE

If our social evils are to be coped with, great, sustained national efforts will be required. Yet our nation is dominated by great business corporations whose aim is profit

[13] *Ibid.*, October 28, 1970.

making, not social regeneration. Moreover, the larger corporations constantly grow bigger by eating their smaller competitors. Mergers used to be related in some way to the business. For example, a steel mill would acquire coal mines. But now we have a tidal wave of conglomerate mergers, under which there is no relationship whatever between the functions of the merged corporations. A tractor company will buy a toothbrush company, merely as a means of investing profits to earn more profits, and the process appears to be endless. Already 102 gigantic corporations control 48 per cent of the assets and 53 per cent of the profits of all U.S. manufacturing firms, and conglomerate expansion proceeds constantly.

Will these colossal companies feel that a great and expensive crusade must be made to rehabilitate our national life, to eliminate its great social evils? We are also at the point where our oil industries have nearly achieved a "total conglomerate" of U.S. energy supplies, including coal. Also the big tax breaks upon which the oil industry builds its huge monopoly are defended by controlling politicians in Congress.

Reform of Congress Required. Certainly we cannot hope to rebuild our national life on anything like an enduring basis without genuine reform in the methods of doing business in the Congress, especially the seniority system, which enables committees to be dominated by elderly chairmen from safe districts, often rural and usually from the South. In the Senate, seniority control is not a rule but a rigid custom, subject to change if there is enough popular pressure against conservative inaction, and against alliances with the military-industrial complex. In the House, the strangling power of the Rules Committee over all legislation is especially at issue. These two roadblocks against far-reaching reform, among others, must be removed if we are to cope with our internal dangers.

Is America Finished? Our continued failure to deal with our deep-seated problems leads some to conclude that America is finished. Professor Andrew Hacker, of Cornell University, has recently published a book, *The End of the American Era,* in which he makes the basic judgment that unwillingness to spend for public needs is a main cause of our social decay. He feels that we are "about to join other nations which were once prepossessing and are now little more than plots of bounded terrain."

This may well prove to be true, but it need not be. As Anthony Lewis has said: "No one should underestimate the energies that would be released, the hopes reborn, the idealism renewed if we were to get out of Vietnam."[14] This would indeed give us a new lease on life, but unfortunately the evidence indicates that President Nixon has no intention of really getting out of Vietnam. He intends to keep on withdrawing our combat troops gradually until the 1972 election, but to leave a powerful garrison of other kinds of troops—especially the devastating Air Force—to maintain our current tyrants Thieu and Ky in power and to hold strategic areas of South Vietnam whatever happens. Thus the great Vietnamese debilitation promises to continue indefinitely, at least semi-paralyzing our efforts to save ourselves internally.

Our difficulty is that in President Nixon the old hard-liner is likely at any time to prevail over the new engineer who is apparently reducing our commitments to police

[14] *Nashville Tennessean,* May 12, 1970.

the world. As *Newsweek* put it, on December 14, 1970, "In moments of crisis the brinksman of the 1950's seems to overwhelm the brakeman of the 70's. The path of American disengagement has been studded with unexpected lunges in the other direction—the invasion of Cambodia, the threat to intervene in Jordan and the recent bombing of North Vietnam. Last week the Administration turned away from withdrawal again. Overriding a recommendation by Secretary of Defense Melvin Laird that the United States cut its NATO manpower commitment, Washington promised to maintain American troop strength in Europe."

Our deep national predicament is that Mr. Nixon thinks the loss of South Vietnam would be a national defeat, instead of a grave national mistake. "There flourished the illusion of American omnipotence, the fantastic notion that one nation could act as global policeman," said Walter Lippmann on December 14, continuing: "When the Vietnamese war ends—pray without a catastrophe—there will be only one salve for our wounds, for our pride, for our honor and for our dignity. Honesty and no pretenses. It is to recognize the mistake as being a mistake, to refrain from pretending that it was not a mistake, and to find the remedy in the universal human knowledge that to err is human."

Youth Repelled. While we wait for a leader who will put Vietnam and the control of Southeast Asia behind him and turn wholeheartedly to rebuilding our national life, there are many attempts among us to chart a better way of life. A large number of our best youth, and from the best families, have withdrawn from the society that has come into such disarray. Many reject the prospect of a life spent in a corporation, either on the assembly line grind or behind a desk waiting a lifetime for promotions and profits. They prefer to live together in little colonies of hippies.

Back to Anarchism? Others have lost faith in the whole vast apparatus of government and want as little of it as possible. An outstanding example is Karl Hess, who wrote the platform for the Republican National Convention in 1960 and again helped to author it in 1964, staying on as Senator Goldwater's speech writer in the ensuing campaign. Surely conservative credentials could not be better, yet today Hess has become an anarchist and we are told reliably that "the graying ex-aides of the elder Senator Robert Taft now write anarchist articles for *The Libertarian Forum.*"

Hess argues to frequent audiences that militarism and welfarism have brought us the garrison state and stagnation. He seeks to restore neighborhood government by boycotting and resisting all higher authority. He traces his own personal rejection to Vietnam, where "we trusted Washington with enormous powers to fight global communism." "We were wrong," he says, "as Taft foresaw when he opposed NATO." We got the killing of a million and a half helpless peasants in Vietnam, "just as impersonally as Stalin exterminated the Kulaks." He found, too, that even a large audience of Catholic girls in a Washington, D.C., college agreed with him in a matter-of-fact way that American society is bankrupt, and they peppered him with questions for four hours.[15]

New Consciousness Emerging. Charles A. Reich, professor of law at Yale, has created something of a sensation

[15] James Boyd, "From Far Right to Far Left and Farther with Karl Hess," The New York Times *Magazine,* December 6, 1970.

with his book *The Greening of America,* in which he agrees that "Day-to-day events leave us with a feeling of chaos; it seems as if we must be powerless spectators at the decline and fall of our country." This is due basically to the "corrosive exploitation" of the Corporate State under which we live, an amalgamation of "both private and public structures," especially big business and big government. What our survival demands, Reich says, is "a new consciousness which will assert rational control over the industrial system and the Corporate State."

This new consciousness, which he calls Consciousness III, "is at last emerging—the spontaneous outgrowth of the fears and hopes of the new generation." It is rational to refuse to become an instrument of the war that is "mindlessly destroying the land, country and people of South East Asia." And if the Corporate State "wants its citizens identically boxed and packaged . . . it makes sense to wear long hair and beards and clothes that constitute a refusal to be regimented." The result is "the bloom of renewed life." There is new hope, "for young people have rediscovered a future, where until recently no future could even be imagined."[16]

[16] *New York Times,* October 21, 22, 1970.

See the remarkable article on corporate responsibility by Hazel Anderson, "Politics by Other Means," in *The Nation,* December 14, 1970. This is one of the most important and surprising articles this writer has read in many years. It describes the many ways by which post-Nader citizen groups are bringing pressure to bear on the corporations, even the greatest, to exercise social responsibility even at the expense of profits.

The powerful ways in which the corporations influence Congress are explained and many cases of successful court action in the public interest are cited. A "new body of legal doctrine of corporate responsibility is steadily emerging." Also campaigns among stockholders are educating the top executives. For example, the Campaign to Make General Motors Responsible did not get its proposals adopted in the annual stockholders'

More Thinking and Action from Below. Arthur Nafta-lin, a four-term mayor of Minneapolis and professor of public affairs at the University of Minnesota, finds the new consciousness which our young people have of a better way of life a thing of great hope—hope of coping with "the horrendous waste of our resources in arms and SST's" and "the inhuman neglect of human necessities." He calls for the consolidation of the "jumble of munici-palities and counties and special districts" into regional governments, a step ahead already taken at Nashville, Tennessee, as a means of helping us to cope with the Corporate State.[17]

In a striking book, *Future Shock*, Alvin Toffler main-tains that "What we are witnessing is the beginning of the final breakup of industrialism and, with it, the col-lapse of technocratic planning." Looking toward a society in which there is less "top-down" thinking and action, democracy at the lower levels "becomes not a political luxury, but a primal necessity."[18]

Encouragingly, too, we find successful examples of new initiatives by our young people, from the bottom upward. The outstanding example is the case of Ralph Nader, a young lawyer who has become the leader of the safety and consumer movements. Using orthodox methods he has "filed lawsuits, testified before congressional com-

---

meeting, but it forced the company to mobilize more than five million shares against them.

Examples of successful local-action assaults against corporations are given and the growing weight of anti-pollution campaigns is explained. One big company is setting up "an internal social accounting system."

This article with its convincing evidence of a whole new field for politi-cal action, in the broadest sense, should be read widely. It gives hope that citizens everywhere can help to reform our society on new fronts, while exerting their influence through traditional legislative channels.

[17] *New York Times*, November 14, 1970.

[18] *Future Shock*, New York, 1970, pp. 420–21.

mittees, solicited stockholders' proxies, and lobbied journalists and politicians." He is accurate and has the facts.
Recently he won an out-of-court settlement from General
Motors, one of our mightiest corporations, for $425,000.
He has also defeated the meat lobby, to achieve a drastic
improvement in meat inspection standards, and his organization is alert for action on many fronts. Last year
he enlisted 170 graduate students to help conduct investi-
gations and he may well "alter the balance between public and private power and perhaps transform the ways in
which major corporations make their decisions." Observing that the big corporations have become private governments, he works to bring them under effective public
control—a logical and effective way of dealing with the
Corporate State.[19]

Even the Harvard School of Business Administration
is the source of imaginative efforts by its students to "do
their own thing." One of its recent graduates has a thriv-
ing consulting company, already employing fifteen of his
fellows, which stands ready to help its clients do what
it recommends. They don't want to wait twenty years to
rise to a job on the management-decision level. "They
want the privilege and excitement of making up their
own minds now."[20]

PERILS SHARED WITH THE WORLD

Behind all of the great problems and perils which we
have considered, and which must be grappled with, loom
three great menaces which must be dealt with on a world

[19] William V. Shannon, *New York Times*, August 23, 1970.
[20] John Chamberlain, *Nashville Tennessean*, December 8, 1970.

scale—overpopulation, man's destruction of our environment, and the global arms race.

Overpopulation. Too many people gives rise to all the other problems. It is clearer every day that populations must be stabilized. It appears that famines will do this in many countries, but here intelligence must be employed. The old goal of constantly exploding population, production, GNPs, and profits has to be abandoned. Otherwise all the dangers that menace us internally will quickly become insoluble. The idea of unlimited millions of alienated, lonely people piled higher and higher into our skies obviously invites disaster. The goal of ever larger Gross National Products zooming ever higher into the heavens also defies reality. Our GNP is now a trillion dollars a year, by current inflated prices. At how many trillions does the whole thing collapse? How many million cars, refrigerators, and gadgets of every kind must be produced annually before we are smothered in the old ones that we want to discard? At what point does the ever accelerating poisoning of our air, water, and soil strangle us, literally and finally? Norman E. Borlaug, who has contributed mightily to expanding world food, says that "if world population continues to expand at the same rate, we will destroy the species."

Every brand of common sense tells us we must have a stabilization of population, with allowance for small fluctuations, by whatever means may be necessary, and that we must return to somewhat simpler ways of life. One does not have to depend on some pastoral dream to visualize smaller, livable cities, somewhat more small-town life, and even measures to make farm life more attractive. In that direction restrictions on great farm corporations would help.

Controlling Pollution. If we are to look forward to even
a moderately long national life, the control of pollution
is as clearly imperative. This means, in the first place, the
outlawry of the internal combustion engine in a few
years. It may irk us somewhat to travel the roads in
electric or steam-engined cars, but no other step would
help us more to persist on this planet awhile, if we can
also perfect municipal power plants that will reduce or
eliminate pollution. We shall encounter the resistance of
every kind of corporation which finds it easier to foul
our air, waters, and soils than to take remedial measures
that will be expensive, but the will of the American people to live must prevail over the convenience and profits
of the corporations. Yet this will not happen while the
corporations that are responsible for the pollution dominate the anti-pollution boards in thirty-five states.[21]

Many nations are rapidly becoming pollution-
conscious. This worldwide trend is encouraging and may
save us, provided the United Nations is given power and
means to coordinate and lead a worldwide struggle to
rescue our environment and to bring into line the countries that insist on continuing pollution. Here, too, populations of manageable size are essential to success.

The Final Arms Race—and Absurdity. Everywhere,
also, there must be insistence on the reduction of arms
burdens and budgets. But nowhere else is the need so
urgent as it is here, where such an enormous part of the
national budget goes for something called defense, in a
time when defense has ceased to be possible. What does
it matter whether a war with Russia, or China, would

[21] A nationwide survey made by the *New York Times* and reported
in its issue of December 7, 1970.

mean the death of two thirds or only half of the people on both sides?

Of course people who still believe in something called power, even after Vietnam, will insist that armed forces be large, and while other powers arm heavily we will feel it essential to do so, but we may have only a few years in which to control and greatly reduce armaments. The nuclear physicist Herbert York, who has followed the domination of nuclear weapon technology since its birth during World War II, has warned us in his book *Race to Oblivion* that we are not far from "the ultimate absurdity."[22]

This final absurdity "lies in the fact that in the United States (and doubtless in the Soviet Union) the power to decide whether or not doomsday has arrived is in the process of passing from statesmen and politicians to lower level officers and technicians and, eventually, to machines." In other words, we cannot wait a few minutes for the President to decide whether a missile attack is in the skies, we must leave it to a computer or other miracle machine to push the button and release our own clouds of counterattacking missiles.

We do not have much time left in which to really achieve arms limitation and stability, and in which to disarm our minds of the delusion that some other government is plotting our instant death. This, too, is an urgent matter in which all citizens must take a hand. In York's words, "If we are to avoid oblivion, if we are to reject the ultimate absurdity, then all of us, not just the current 'in' group of experts and technicians, must involve ourselves in creating the policies and making the decisions necessary to do so."[23]

[22] *Race to Oblivion*, New York, 1970, p. 228.
[23] *Ibid.*, p. 239.

Another of our original nuclear scientists, Ralph E. Lapp, who has become a top authority on the military-industrial complex, warned in a recent book, *Arms Beyond Doubt*, "that we have overreached ourselves in our quest for security and that by so doing we have led to an escalation of the arms race. . . . We arm not just beyond doubt, but beyond belief. We arm for a war in which all men are victims."[24]

Even if the system of nuclear deterrence does not trigger the use of the hydrogen bomb it will still destroy us, for, as Joseph Lyford, President of the Fund for Peace, said in his 1970 annual report: ". . . it has set loose forces which are irrevocably undermining the human condition . . . by so distorting the economies of nations and the psychology of their citizens that the diverse and delicate political processes of all the world's nations are showing signs of disintegration," so that the arms race, "if unchecked, will eventually bring about the extinction of human societies as effectively as if they had been subjected to mass nuclear violence."

Japan and West Germany have led all the world since 1945 in prosperity, exactly because they have spent little on the sterile, destructive business of militarism.

We Can Change Course

By leading the procession on this disastrous road, and by engaging in the long, bloody absurdity of the Vietnam War, we have promoted our own disintegration to the stage where it may escape control. In his very thoughtful book *Man's Past: Man's Future*, Stephen Raushenbush

[24] *Arms Beyond Doubt*, New York, 1970, pp. 15, 193.

drives home the poignancy of our decline: "In the early twentieth century the United States was still the great and envied hope of the world. By the 1960s it had become the most watched, most criticized and occasionally most feared world power. By then it had begun to show several of these signs of outward arrogance and unbearable inner stress which marked the disintegration of other major cultures in the past. These warning signals flared at the very moment when it eclipsed all the potentials of other historic societies: no other culture ever had its capacity to enrich or, alternatively, to destroy life and hope throughout the whole world; no other ever had so many billions of people ultimately dependent, in one way or another, on its wishes, its decisions, its example."[25]

Shall we fail humanity and ourselves?

It is not foreordained. We can still recover our sanity and common sense. We can still employ our great resources for rebuilding what we have so blindly let decay. We can by degrees restore our world leadership in labors for living, instead of dying. For many decades we were a beacon to all the world, a free society engaged in constructive endeavors.

It can be so again, if we move quickly and strongly to recover our heritage. We can succeed, especially if we make use of the zeal and leadership of our youth in moving into new directions. The Scranton Commission pointed the way, saying: "A nation driven to use weapons of war against its youth is a nation on the edge of chaos. . . . A nation that has lost the allegiance of its youth is a nation that has lost its future."

[25] *Man's Past: Man's Future,* New York, 1970.

EPILOGUE

The most poignant sentence spoken about our struggles for survival came from the wisdom of Senator Mike Mansfield. This nation, he said, is too young to die. This might well become our rallying cry.

ABOUT THE AUTHOR

D. F. Fleming is Emeritus Professor of International Relations at Vanderbilt University. Since his retirement in 1961 he has taught at the University of Arizona, the California State College at Los Angeles, Simon Fraser University at Vancouver, B.C., and Middle Tennessee State University at Murfreesboro.

In recent years he has lectured widely in the West, at the University of South Florida and Northwestern University as well as the colleges in Nashville.

Earlier he was a columnist for the *Nashville Tennessean,* 1934–37; radio commentator for WSM in Nashville, 1939–47; three times an observer at the League of Nations in Geneva during its great crises; twice a member at the Institute for Advanced Studies in Princeton; and Fulbright Lecturer at Cambridge University in England and at the School of International Studies in New Delhi, India. He has been President of the Southern Political Science Association and Vice-President of the American Political Science Association.

He was a member of Bernard Baruch's staff during

our atomic energy negotiations with the U.S.S.R. in 1946.

About the most noted of Dr. Fleming's ten books, *The Cold War and Its Origins, 1917–1960*, which Doubleday published in 1961, with five later printings, a student at the University of Michigan wrote: "For many of us reading this book has been a central life experience." When his book *The Origins and Legacies of World War I* was published by Doubleday in 1968, the famous Swedish author Gunnar Myrdal wrote: "I have been reading the book with great excitement. I think it is an excellent book which should have the widest spread."

GEORGE ALLEN & UNWIN LTD

Head Office:
London: 40 Museum Street, W.C.1

Trade orders and enquiries:
Park Lane, Hemel Hempstead, Herts

Athens: 7 Stadiou Street, Athens 125
Barbados: Rockley New Road, St. Lawrence 4
Bombay: 103/5 Fort Street, Bombay 1
Calcutta: 285J Bepin Behari Ganguli Street, Calcutta 12
Dacca: Alico Building, 18 Motijheel, Dacca 2
Hornsby, N.S.W. Cnr. Bridge Road and Jersey Street, 2077
Ibadan: P.O. Box 62
Johannesburg: P.O. Box 23134, Joubert Park
Karachi: Karachi Chambers, McLoed Road, Karachi 2
Lahore: 22 Falettis' Hotel, Egerton Road
Madras : 2/18 Mount Road, Madras 2
Manila: P.O. Box 157, Quezon City, D–502
Mexico: Serapio Rendon 125, Mexico 4, D.F.
Nairobi: P.O. Box 30583
New Delhi: 4/21–22B Asaf Ali Road, New Delhi 1
Ontario: 2330 Midland Avenue, Agincourt
Singapore: 248C–6 Orchard Road, Singapore 9
Tokyo: C.P.O. Box 1728, Tokyo 100–91
Wellington: P.O. Box 1467, Wellington, New Zealand